GIRLS'
WILL BE
GIRLS

GIRLS WILL BE GIRLS

DRESSING UP, PLAYING PARTS AND DARING TO ACT DIFFERENTLY

EMER O'TOOLE

Copyright © Emer O'Toole 2015

The right of Emer O'Toole to be identified as the author
of this work has been asserted in accordance with
the Copyright, Designs and Patents Act 1988.

This edition first published in Great Britain in 2015
by Orion
an imprint of the Orion Publishing Group Ltd
Orion House, 5 Upper St Martin's Lane,
London WC2H 9EA
An Hachette UK Company

1 3 5 7 9 10 8 6 4 2

The author and publisher are grateful to the following for permission to
quote: 'I Enjoy Being a Girl' © Copyright 1958 by Imagen Music CV.
Used by permission of Williamson Music, a division of
Rodgers & Hammerstein: An Imagen Company.

A CIP catalogue record for this book
is available from the British Library.

Trade Paperback ISBN: 978 1 4091 4873 9

Typeset at The Spartan Press Ltd,
Lymington, Hants

Printed and bound by the CPI Group (UK) Ltd,
Croydon, CR0 4YY

The Orion Publishing Group's policy is to use papers
that are natural, renewable and recyclable and made
from wood grown in sustainable forests. The logging and
manufacturing processes are expected to conform to the
environmental regulations of the country of origin.

Every effort has been made to fulfil requirements with regard
to reproducing copyright material. The author and publisher will
be glad to rectify any omissions at the earliest opportunity.

www.orionbooks.co.uk

For my brothers, Ronan and Ciarán.
Never liked ye.

'...gender is an act which has been rehearsed, much as a script survives the particular actors who make use of it, but which requires individual actors in order to be actualised and reproduced as reality once again.'   Judith Butler[1]

'It diminishes a fem(me), all fem(me)s, to talk about a "fem(me)" identity in itself. How could that be? Fem(me) is neither an ideal nor a category. She makes a scene, an entrance, an appearance – she steals the show (she is the show) of difference, but she cannot be fixed as a certain effect "in itself." Fem(me) is always inter-actionable, never onanistic or narcissistic. Mirrors are not the pool in which she drowns; they are the instrument or metaphor of her essential irony.'   Lisa Duggan and Kathleen McHugh[2]

'I believe with my wholeheartmindbody that girls constitute a revolutionary soul force that can and will change the world for real.'   Kathleen Hanna[3]

CONTENTS

INTRODUCTION:

LIGHTS, CAMERA, ACTION

'For the things we have to learn before we can do them, we learn by doing them, e.g. men become builders by building and lyreplayers by playing the lyre; so too we become just by doing just acts, temperate by doing temperate acts, brave by doing brave acts.'

Aristotle[4]

A CHARACTER STUDY

I'm sixteen, and I have rudely interrupted the school choir's rendition of *Silent Night* by passing out and falling from the top step of the soprano rostrum onto the unsuspecting scrunchies of the girls below.

I don't know if you've ever fainted, but, experientially speaking, it's pretty interesting. Of course, it's hard to concentrate on its interestingness when you're a sixteen-year-old girl who's just made a dick of herself in front of the entire school, but never mind. Fainting is like watching fuzzy black clouds slowly encroach on your vision from the outside in. By the time you're aware that there's only a small and shrinking puddle of light through which to find the world, you're not entirely sure whether you're dreaming or awake. Then you decide dreaming. Then you wake up on top of Patricia Houlihan, who is saying 'Jesus Christ', although this ejaculation may well get her detention for blasphemy. (Detention for blasphemy is not unheard of. In fact, I only ever got detention once, and it was for answering 'Jesus' when my history teacher asked me who founded the Gaelic Athletic Association.)

When you are peeled off poor Patricia, a kindly vice-principal takes you outside and says nice things like 'it was very stuffy in there.' You are both well aware, however, from the sight and sound of your bluish, crackling and emaciated wrists, that the problem is not a lack of oxygen, but a lack of foodstuffs other than Weetabix, soup, apples and half of whatever your mother nightly begs you to eat for dinner. The vice-principal asks if you want to call your parents. You say no – it's almost home time anyways. When the refrain of *Silent Night* re-establishes itself, making you cringe like a poked hedgehog, the vice-principal says, with the psychic intuition lifelong observers of teenage anxiety possess, 'no one will remember after the holidays.' And that, to the best of my recollection, is what happens when you faint.

This is a book about how we perform our genders. It is also, in large part, about the body – because our bodies are used to define us and socialise us. I've started with an image of my body falling because the event is a kind of performance. Perhaps not an intentional or conscious one, but a performance all the same – a part of the character I assumed to play the part of 'girl'. The fall is not a benign, sweet or giggly enactment of girldom: it's a harmful one, a sad one; it's a performance that shows we need a new script. While lots of people, such as my erstwhile vice-principal, can recognise this need, no one seems to know how the lines got written in the first place, let alone how to begin writing new ones. And so the problem is ignored. The show, after all, must go on.

This is also, often, a book about my own experiences, which are personal and subjective. I'm aware that my life does not hold universal relevance. I hope it's still worthwhile, however, to share the lessons I've learned as a woman who likes to play with social expectation, who gave up trying not to embarrass herself years ago, and who has spent a lot of time thinking about the pleasures, pitfalls and contradictions of performing her girldom and her womanhood.

A brief note on what this book is not: it isn't a scientific book about neurological differences between men and women. There are lots of excellent publications on the subject out there – I particularly like Lise Eliot's *Blue Brain, Pink Brain* and Cordelia Fine's *Delusions of Gender*, both of which are rigorous, entertaining and written by women with PhDs in neuroscience.

Based on my reading of Eliot, Fine and others, my understanding of differences between male and female brains is this: there are small innate biological differences between men and women's psychologies, which our treatment of people in male bodies and female bodies conditions into significant and oftentimes worrisome gaps. The brain is plastic, and while both nature and nurture affect the people we come to be, it is our nature, as humans, to be nurtured.

That's why thinking of gender as a kind of performance – as a series of acts that can, with conscious intent, be rewritten – is an idea with revolutionary power. If we can change these performances, we can transform what it means to be male or female in our society.

I have a PhD in theatre studies (a fact that was predictable from about the time I was three years old). This makes me the kind of doctor you least want to be sat next to should you be having a heart attack on a plane, but the one you most want to be beside should you want to spend the flight downing G&Ts and humming show tunes. Joking aside, I believe in the importance of studying performance – onstage and off – as a way of understanding human behaviour and identity.

But back to my blue-fingered, crackle-boned teenage incarnation. Why was I starving myself? From the outside, self-enforced hunger looks like a pretty masochistic way for anyone to treat their body. If my teachers thought my parents had been restricting me to 1000 calories or under every day for six months – until my periods stopped, my extremities were blue and I had more hair stuck to the shoulders of my school jumper than to my scalp – they'd have called social services: it'd be abuse. So, when someone behaves like this, it's logical – in our individualistic society – to assume that self-starvation equals self-loathing and self-harm. And for some people it does. But I did not hate myself and I didn't want to hurt myself.

I've had family, friends and lovers try to convince me that my eating disorder was the result of problems at home, or confusion about my sexuality, or exam stress, or an unfulfilled childhood desire for a pet stick insect, and I've listened and seriously considered all of this (*did* I subconsciously want a stick insect?). But these explanations seem removed from the simple truth: I was starving myself because I wanted to be very thin.

In Aristotle's *Nichomachean Ethics*, the Ancient Greek philosopher suggests that happiness is the only thing that a person can desire for its own sake. If I ask you why you want money, you might answer, 'to buy diamonds'. If I ask why you want diamonds, you might answer, 'because they're beautiful'. If I ask why you want beauty, you might reply, 'because it makes me happy'. But it doesn't make any sense to ask why you want happiness. Happiness is the ultimate end – the only thing you can desire for its own sake and nothing more.

My teenage self would have wrecked Aristotle's Hellenic head. Imagine: it's 340BC, and sixteen-year-old me patters past the Acropolis on spindly legs. I bump into Arty boy, and, even though he believes that people with vaginas are too irrational to be able to think properly,[5] he condescends to speak with me. 'My my, Emer,' he says, 'you do look like you need a sizeable chunk of feta. Pray, why are you starving yourself?' 'Well, friend Aristotle,' I reply, 'it's because I want to be thin.' 'Ah yes, but *why* do you want to be thin?' says Aristotle. 'Girls should be thin,' I answer. 'Do you not desire to be thin in order to attract a virile young Athenian male?' 'Mmmm, no, I have a boyfriend. He thinks I should put on some weight.' 'Do you not desire to be thin so that you can embark on a successful modelling career? Not here in Athens, of course – for aesthetic and practical purposes our sculptors prefer women with fewer bones in high relief – but perhaps in some twisted foreign or future clime, where emaciated women are venerated?' 'Mmmm, no, I want to be a doctor when I grow up.'

Aristotle is getting a bit pissed off at this point, but he doesn't like to let on when his tunic's being tugged the wrong way. 'See now,' he helpfully explains, 'every desire or need can be explained in terms of another desire or need, until finally we reach the ultimate end: happiness. Yes? So, in what way do you think that being thin will make you happy?' 'Because it's good to be thin? Y'know, like the girls on TV?' It is at this point that Aristotle storms off home and writes that in women the deliberative capacity lacks force. Femaledom suffers for his observations for millennia. Sorry.

Our complex brains mean that we are all philosophers. For Aristotle, because humans are rational by their nature, happiness comes, in large part, from thinking about how best to act and, based on this, living a good life. Being in good health, having enough money and allowing ourselves pleasures contributes to our happiness, but – because we're thinkers – we can't really be fulfilled unless we're acting in ways that we believe are valuable.

Aristotle says that it's through carrying out brave acts that we become brave, generous acts that we become generous, or just acts that we become just. The actions we perform over time create our characters, our sense of worth and our happiness. For Aristotle, we should behave in ways that are 'virtuous'. And what's particularly satisfying about his idea of virtue is that it isn't the same rule for everyone, but, rather, people have to figure out the ways of acting that are best for themselves.

This theory of happiness might have been written approximately 2,350 years ago, but it still has a lot to teach us. What Aristotle understands as 'virtue', I understand as thinking about our social roles and acting in ways that will create the kind of world we'd like to see. But this is hard, because we receive a lot of 'common sense' ideas about the parts we *should* play from our families, friends and from society more broadly; we are rewarded for playing these parts, and we have to deal with the fall-out if we act differently.

Teenage me wanted to be very thin because she knew that, in her society, it was good to be very thin. It almost didn't make sense to ask why. All my girl friends wanted to be thin. All the women in magazines and on television were thin. Fat people were to be mocked and/or pitied. And yes, my diet went too far (possibly because I was small anyways so it took me less time to become unhealthy), but was my 'anorexia' really all that different to my friends' yo-yoing and guilt-drenched relationships with their bodies and with food? We were all trying out for the same star role: that of the skinny chick.

I'd been socialised to believe that women should be thin. I learned this belief early from the images and attitudes around me; I internalised it, and while I might have been able to question it on a theoretical level, in my practical, day-to-day experience it was an incontrovertible truth. Being thin was a way of performing my society's ideal of femininity. My friends and I were acting in ways we thought were good, presuming that we'd get pleasure from being considered beautiful, without stopping to think about how these ways of acting were affecting us and the world around us: without properly considering that it was possible to act differently.

Being thin wasn't the only way of performing my society's ideal of femininity. I also needed a padded bra because my breasts were small, unacceptably un-spherical and adorned with deeply provocative nipples (the contours of which it was necessary to disguise); I needed make-up because my face was plain without it; fake tan because my skin was not an appropriate shade of caramel; and razors because my body hair was disgusting. I was socialised into all these beliefs, and not only did I internalise them, I shamed women who didn't conform to them and enjoyed the praise I received for performing my pin-limbed, padded, painted and plucked female identity.

I also learned other, less tangible attitudes towards how women should act from my home life, school life and exposure to media and culture: attitudes to child-rearing, parenthood and housework; attitudes about who belongs in positions of power; attitudes to language; and attitudes to sexuality.

My mother usually started the day with an hour of ironing before getting my brothers and me off to school. I used to like waking up to the comforting creak of the ironing board and the clean, steamy smell in the kitchen. After convincing her three kids to get out of bed, providing them with uncrumpled school uniforms, breakfasting them, packing their lunches, ensuring that they were clad in outer layers proficient to external temperature and moisture and bundling them off down the road to school, Mum would go to work in Galway City. When we were younger, we had a babysitter who was there when we got home in the afternoon, feeding us and keeping the place tidy. When we got older, we didn't, and we'd all tumble in, leave a hurricane's worth of chaos in the kitchen, and plonk ourselves in front of *Home and Away*. Mum would return to a filthy house and unresponsive offspring. Then she'd get angry and shout at us, before cleaning up and starting to cook our dinner. My father didn't cook and did almost no housework.

As I got older and developed the curious capacity of empathy for one's parents, I fell into a pattern of trying to have the house nice for Mum when she came home. This meant that I cleaned up after my brothers a lot. (Until we got a PlayStation, Ciarán – the youngest – could sometimes be persuaded to help out, but Ronan – the eldest – was impossible.) Now, if you'd asked me if I was tidying up after my brothers and father because I was a girl, I'd have said, 'no, I'm doing it because I don't want Mum to be upset when she gets home.' But I clearly learned that it was my role to do this work from somewhere. And my brothers learned that they were justified in sitting around on their arses from somewhere too.

When I watched the news at night, the vast majority of political leaders making speeches and decisions were male. My parents and teachers told me that I could be anything I wanted to be, but that message was silently contradicted by the power structures I was becoming aware existed around me. Positions of power were primarily male positions.

On television, men middle-aged or older presented chat

shows alongside young, beautiful female colleagues. The implication, again unspoken, was clear: the men were there due to their talents, and the women (even if also talented) due to their looks. It was not enough to be clever and dedicated – if I wanted success, I needed to be pretty too.

From the language I read in books, studied in class and heard spoken around me I learned that, collectively, people made up humanity: that *fellow* feeling led to the *brotherhood* of *man*.* I learned that in cases where a pronoun was needed and the gender of the subject was unclear, I should use 'he' or 'him'. In business studies class, I learned to address letters to 'Dear Sirs', or 'Dear Sir or Madam', never 'Dear Madams', and never 'Dear Madam or Sir'. I learned that adult men were Misters and remained Misters their lives long, while women would transmogrify from Miss to Missus when someone liked it enough to put a ring on it. I learned that when two people got married, the woman took her husband's name, as did all the small *human*s she grew in her tummy. I learned to use language that privileged male experience and identity – language that put women second.

I heard the terms 'girl' and 'woman' used as insults, and the term 'man' used as praise. I learned a plethora of words for women who had lots of sexual partners – slag, slapper, slut, floozy, tramp, tart, loose, easy, prozzy, bike, whore

---

* I first came across this phrase reading the Universal Declaration of Human Rights. Eleanor Roosevelt, who co-wrote the declaration, is a personal hero and she had the excuse that she was writing in the fifties. 4 Non Blondes, however, as '90s pop rock starlets, have no such excuse, and we should all endeavour to change the lyrics to (the timeless classic) 'What's Up' whenever some cheeseball (me) starts playing it at parties.

– and one for men: gigolo, which always seemed to carry an air of humorous accomplishment somehow. And I learned the worst thing you could say, the very worst word of all, was cunt. I learned to talk about female sexual behaviour and the female body differently – more pejoratively – to the way I spoke about male equivalents.

Like almost all Irish people who grow up in the Republic, I went to Catholic school, and learned to bless myself in the name of the Father, the Son and the Holy Spirit. I learned that divinity and authority were male, and Mary, the mortal mother of God, was blessed because she was a virgin. Every Sunday I went to mass, and watched a man on the altar (in a position from which women are forbidden) tell me how to behave. I learned that to be godly meant to accept the inferior position of women. (I'm an atheist now, thank God.)

In sex ed (what little of it we had), we learned that abortion was wrong, and that abstinence was the only sure-fire way to prevent pregnancy. Three girls in my co-ed year of about 120 were pregnant before our final exams. That's one in twenty. That's five per cent. Women have no access to abortion in Ireland. We learned that the choice fourteen Irish women make every day – to travel to England and terminate a pregnancy – was morally wrong. We learned that women are immoral.

And when it came to sexuality, I grew up surrounded by ignorance: homophobia, misogyny and slut shaming. I came from a progressive household compared to most of my friends (my mother works in sexual health, so she's pretty clued in), but I distinctly remember Mum saying, 'of course I'll love you if you're gay. But I hope you're not, because it'd make your life so much more difficult.' Which is really very sweet and maternal, but, combined with the regressive attitudes of the West of Ireland in the nineties in general, didn't exactly instil me with confidence in exploring my sexuality outside of sanctioned boy-meets-girl parameters. I learned to act like a straight girl.

I knew how to perform my female identity in the way my society deemed best. Other girls, from different nations, cultures, classes or races learn different, but intersecting, versions of this role. I was well into adulthood before I became aware that I was in a carefully scripted show. Even after I began to see the lights, the curtains, the expectant audience singing along, I didn't stop playing my ordained part. I continued to sport the compulsory costume and choreography of womanhood, repeating the appropriate feminine actions that created my appropriately feminine character. I'd only learned one set of lines. I had no idea what would happen if I started making up new ones as I went along.

This book began with an image of my body falling, because this book is going to take the body down and rebuild it. From the second the doctor shouts 'it's a girl' our bodies are used to define us, to dictate which of our behaviours are acceptable, and how it is acceptable for others to treat us.[6] Our bodies are coded and costumed to turn us into easily identifiable men and women, creating artificial divisions in society and limiting the identities that people of any gender feel confident performing. So let's start thinking about our performances of womanhood – where they came from, whose agendas they serve – and let's start writing new scripts.

CHAPTER ONE:

REHEARSING

All the world's a stage,
And all the men and women merely players;
They have their exits and their entrances,
And one man in his time plays many parts

Shakespeare (Jacques from *As You Like It*)

I ENJOY BEING A GIRL

I am a nine-year-old diva, and my Saturday stage school is putting on its annual end-of-year variety show in Our Holy Mother of Mercy school hall. It's a high-octane event – a night on which memories are made, dreams broken. Rehearsals have been intensive, and butterflies on amphetamine now flutter in the tummies of Galway's most precocious little brats. Backstage is a heady mélange of fake tan, hair spray, ripped tights, orangey pound-shop foundation sticks and about a hundred gigantic egos in tiny human vessels.

This year I've been chosen to sing a duet with a boy called Paul (who I do NOT fancy, leave me alone he's NOT my boyfriend and I HAVE to sit on his knee 'cause that's the CHOREOGRAPHY). We are Hansel and Gretel, and, as we wait in the wings dressed in what's supposed to be, respect-ively, lederhosen and a mini milkmaid outfit (but is actually, respectively, braces and school trousers tucked into Paul's dad's socks and some random flowery dress), we watch the girls from the class above perform their chorus number.

And it's strange, because I don't remember much about my Hansel and Gretel song (other than that I believed it completely unnecessary for me to have to sit on Paul's knee), but I've always remembered the piece that went on before it. In it, about twenty little girls in various shades of pink sported fake pearls, frills (ex-doilies), heads full of curlers, and faces full of make-up. They sang and danced to 'I Enjoy Being a Girl' from the 1958 Rodgers and Hammerstein musical *Flower Drum Song*.

> *I'm a girl, and by me that's only great!*
> *I am proud that my silhouette is curvy,*
> *That I walk with a sweet and girlish gait*
> *With my hips kind of swively and swervy.*

The little starlets (well, the ones who, faced with their expectant public, could remember to do anything other than stare like doomed rabbits into the spotlights) twirled and simpered in parodies of womanhood: waggling their hips, primping their pouts, blowing kisses and posing for imaginary wolf whistles.

> *I adore being dressed in something frilly*
> *When my date comes to get me at my place.*
> *Out I go with my Joe or John or Billy,*
> *Like a filly who is ready for the race!*

In the audience, mums and dads attempted to photograph their daughters at moments when they appeared to be in step with the other children. Some had to be physically restrained from running on stage to rescue little Róisín or Maeve, who had emerged from her light-induced stupor only to start sobbing. Most, however, smiled at the silliness of the spectacle – at these fillies, so far from ready for racing, enacting faux-flirty caricatures of outmoded womanhood. This was a song from the fifties, after all, and, even in the (not exactly cosmopolitan) nineties West of Ireland, we were well past these clichés of 'being a girl', weren't we?

Yet, I'm not so sure, age nine, that I got the irony. Childhood is, in many ways, a rehearsal for adulthood, and I don't think I understood that the image of womanhood sent up in this song was not one I should someday hope to perform. The messages I was getting from the world around me seemed to indicate that to be proud of being a girl meant to be proud of being pretty and sweet. During the 'girls/boys are better than boys/girls' wars in which feisty small humans so enthusiastically engage, I didn't seem to have much ammo. Boys were bigger, boys were stronger and, in my occasional analyses of the incomprehensible world of adults, it did look as though boys were more likely to be in charge.

If I was proud of being a girl, what was I supposed to be proud of? If I liked being a girl (which I was pretty sure I did; I mean, I wouldn't have swapped or anything), what was it that I was supposed to like? I think I've always believed, perhaps from having two brothers I'm very close to, that boys and girls are the same on the inside. I certainly didn't think that boys were smarter, or girls more emotional. I knew I could add things up as quickly as my big brother, and I knew that boys, brave in public because it was expected of them, were every bit as much cry babies at home.

If boys and girls were more or less the same on the inside, to be proud of being a girl must've meant to be proud of something on the outside. It wasn't being stronger than boys or better at sports (although I was definitely better at climbing trees: a sport for which, sadly, there was little official recognition), so it must be the things that girls do differently – how they dress; how they look. To be proud of being a girl must mean to be proud of all this 'girly' stuff.

> *When I have a brand new hairdo*
> *With my eyelashes all in curl,*
> *I float as the clouds on air do,*
> *I enjoy being a girl!*

As I grew up, my appearance did seem to be of more importance than my brothers'. Take our First Holy Communions, which happened when we were six or seven. My brothers wore nice little trousers and waistcoats, sure, but did they get special white dresses with hoops inside that swung like lampshades and glimmered with crystalline beads? Did they get tiaras or bows for their hair? Did they wear white gloves? Or have little silk purses into which to stuff the tenners pressed into their blesséd (yet greedy) hands by aunties and uncles?

I remember how special all this pomp made me feel.

I remember looking at myself in the mirror and thinking I looked like an angel princess. (Sadly, the angel princess was lacking her two front teeth, making her appear, in truth, less like an angel princess and more like a photographic negative of Bugs Bunny.) In short, I remember learning that self-decoration made me feel special.

> *When men say I'm cute and funny*
> *And my teeth aren't teeth, but pearl,*
> *I just lap it up like honey*
> *I enjoy being a girl!*

It seemed to be largely exterior things that made other people think I was special too. When, holding my mum's hand, one of her friends or acquaintances approached (I have one of those mums who knows everyone), I always knew how the conversation would go:

'Is this yours?'

'It is, yes.'

'Isn't she gorgeous?'

'Well, I think so.'

'She isn't a bit like you.'

'No.'

And, as my mum dealt pleasantly with the backhanded insults, I would smile at the stranger who'd complimented me, not paying much attention really. (This would generally have been the millionth stranger my mother had stopped to talk to in the preceding ten minutes. Sometimes strangers would pile up. It was as if all of Galway was conspiring, yes *conspiring*, to make me late for dance class.)

This stuff penetrated. I didn't realise it for a long time, but the constant adult commentary on the merits of my physical appearance, it penetrated. It taught me to value myself as others seemed to value me: based on being pretty and girly. And, as I got older, I lapped it up like honey. More: I started to crave this attention; to *need* a compliment about my appearance in order to feel good about myself, and to perform actions to procure those compliments – actions, of course, involving clothes, make-up, diets and grooming.

I remembered this facet of my childhood experience following an ostensibly unremarkable event. I was in my early twenties, in the ladies toilet of a tearoom in the Wicklow mountains. I was poking at my painted face, trying to make my chin look more beige or my eyelashes look more individual, when a little girl of about five and an elegant woman (who I'm going to call her Auntie) walked in, seemingly so that Auntie could poke at her own painted face while little girl wee'd. When the child had dutifully piddled and been lifted up to wash her hands, Auntie took down her baby ponytail and re-tied it, pulling dark ringlets from the crown to frame a little face. Then Auntie took out some perfume and sprayed it on the girl's wrists and neck. She straightened up her niece's clothes, smiled into big round eyes and said: 'Now! Aren't you beautiful!?'

There was so much love in those gestures. And the little girl was so happy to be made beautiful and called beautiful by this stylish grown-up, whom she very obviously adored. But when they left the bathroom, as I continued my labours on a particularly inappropriately angled eyelash, I thought 'How is she going to know that her looks are not what matters?' I suddenly remembered all the adults smiling down into my upturned eyes, calling me gorgeous, and I looked at the face in the mirror (a face which, at that point in my life, I felt I had to paint meticulously each and every morning before leaving the house), and in the warmth of all those compliments, I saw harm done.

I'm not saying that, unilaterally, telling a little girl she's beautiful is harmful. But when physical compliments are the default adult interaction with small human females, there is great potential for harm. When rituals of beauty are a primary mode of women showing girl-children love, then of course girls begin to equate their love-worthiness with their looks. After this incident, I started to notice how adults treat little girls. I started to notice how *I* treat little girls.

I have a goddaughter, and she is so very, very beautiful. When I see her, I want to shout 'oh my God she's SO BEAUTIFUL!' And I want to talk about how lovely her princess dress is, and how cute she looks in her little shoes. But she's not a doll. She's five – she doesn't give a shit about shoes. Yet every female adult she meets seems to think shoes are the most important thing to talk to her about. She's at an age where everything's new and everything's interesting, yet these creatures from the womanly realm, who have knowledge of life's mysteries that is boundless compared to her own, keep talking about *shoes*. You know – the things that keep your feet warm. How dull must I seem? And how badly am I failing to teach her what's important: about herself, about women, and about the world?

So now (although I still tell her, of course, that she is beautiful), I try to interact with my goddaughter in much

19

the same way that I interact with her brother: by showing interest in the games she's playing, and asking questions, and telling her how clever and funny she is. I try to steer clear of compliments about her ability to colour between the lines, however, as when in the past I have attempted these her brother has been vocal in his opinion that I am a liar. This valuable lesson in sincerity notwithstanding, I now try to show my admiration for my hilarious, bright and special godchild by complimenting the things she does, not the things she wears.

But now I have another problem: what to buy her for Christmas?

> *I flip when a fellow sends me flowers,*
> *I drool over dresses made of lace,*
> *I talk on the telephone for hours*
> *With a pound and a half of cream upon my face!*

We all know that grown-up ladies flip for flowers, but how did they learn such gymnastics? When you think about it, flower flipping is hardly surprising: we've been rapturously unwrapping gender-specific presents our whole lives.

Visualise: It's Christmas Eve and you are standing in a panic-soiled toyshop trying to find something for your special little girls and boys. All around you, parents are losing their shit, pleading with customer services to please, oh please, let there be one more Furbie, just one, hiding in the dark and emitting scared electronic whimpers at the back of the storeroom. The tills are weakly bleeping in discord, like heartbeat monitors predicting death. Your head is pounding because, entirely against your will, you've spent every night for the last two weeks at inescapable Christmas parties. You only barely recognise the feeling of cold sobriety slithering slug-like over your skin. You are in hell.

The temptation is huge to pick up generic girl present number 347 from the girls' section and generic boy present number 217 from the boys' section and run. The generic girls' present is pink, and has something to do with domestic chores or beauty regimes. The generic boys' present is blue, and has something to do with motor vehicles or gratuitous violence. You briefly consider a giant talking SpongeBob SquarePants, but you've provided enormously irritating *SpongeBob* toys for the last three birthdays and Christmases running, and you may well be fired as godmother if you try that trick again. You lurch, nauseous, from blue aisle to pink aisle, but there's nothing that doesn't make you want to throw up into a temptingly-located doll's pram. You think back. As a child, what did people get you for Christmas?

As if you are drowning, an entire lifetime of presents flashes before your eyes: dolls with magic hair and make-up; pissing effigies of babies; glittery, flower-painted ponies; a weird disembodied life-size head and shoulders with peroxide-blonde hair for the purposes of grooming; handbags; hairbands; non-toxic nail-varnish with an accompanying book about ingenious non-toxic nail varnish patterns; a Fisher-Price kitchen (I still remember the advert, where a little girl wakes her father up with the plastic spoils of her culinary imagination and says 'Breakfast's ready Daddy!');

jewellery making kits; Barbies: PINK, PINK, EVERYTHING PINK.

You break down. You drag yourself to the queue of crazed Furbie-deficient adults at customer services and, when it is your turn, you sob: 'I want a present for the children in my life that is not based on gender stereotypes.' The zombie behind the desk, himself harrowed from dwelling in an underworld that he is financially bound not to quit, suggests a rainbow-coloured xylophone. You fall to your knees and kiss his feet. He tells you that if you do not take your xylophone and go he will call security. You leave, repressing the entire ordeal until the same time next year.

I'm strictly a female female
And my future I hope will be
In the home of a brave and free male
Who'll enjoy being a guy having a girl… like… me.

But there isn't always a xylophone. And sometimes a Barbie is just easier. Sometimes your little loved one desperately *wants* a Barbie. And it's impossible to protect her from the tsunami of pink plastic beautification and domesticity training tools too zealously anyway. What are you going to do? Throw out all her birthday presents after every party?

And, in fact, as Cordelia Fine argues in *Delusions of Gender*, even the most well-meaning, leftie, feminist parents channel and craft their children's gender performances, limiting, in particular, their sons' access to traditionally feminine toys.[7] Further, young children pick up on non-verbal cues such as body language and tone of voice, internalising values that parents might not even know they are imparting. This leads parents who think they're engaged in gender-neutral child-rearing to fall back on biological explanations for their children's toy and game preferences, rather than seeing the deeply embedded attitudes to gender that pervade kids' lives.

Attitudes to female bodies and female worth are pervasive, and little girls learn the lines of womanhood early. The things that we learn to take pleasure from as children condition us into strictly female females. Playtime is a rehearsal. We smear waxy make-up onto the eyelids and puckered mouths of scary doll heads in preparation for the day when we are allowed to start colouring in our own skin. We dress fashion dolls in high heels, which, as soon as the tweens begin, we beg our parents for. Nail varnish and jewellery are permitted early, make-up and sexy clothes later. We long to turn into the leggy, busty princesses on our television screens and in our dollhouses, and when we don't we start performing rituals to make ourselves more closely resemble the impossible ideal.

I hated shopping as a child. I remember being dragged around Penneys (Ireland's pre-Primark) whining like a badly trained Jack Russell and only just resisting the urge to bite strangers' ankles. Yet, in late childhood and my early teens, shopping trips became mother/daughter-bonding time – special hours punctuated with cake in coffee shops – and so I began to enjoy them. I had graduated to a dress rehearsal for womanhood, but the dress rehearsal was really just an extension of the games that went before.

Remember your best friends' bedrooms in your early

teens? Remember the intimate spaces they became for practising the rituals of womanhood: the clothes swapping, the
makeovers, the facemasks, manicures, botched hair curling
and disastrous eyebrow plucking? Remember the newness
of shaving your legs (age thirteen, I taught my eleven-year-
old cousin Saoirse how: a fact with which she threatens to
destroy my feminist writing career on a regular basis); of
periods; of kissing boys?

Bliss, *Sugar* and *Just 17* magazines quizzed us on our
flirting styles and advised us how to get beach bods. I went
on my first diet with my cousin Megan when we were both
twelve. She taught me how to count calories. On the first
day, I ate 1000 and was proud, but Megan was cross with
me, because if you eat too few calories you're not doing it
right. I was by no means an early rider on the bad body
image bandwagon. Ofsted research from 2008 shows that
a third of ten-year-old girls are unhappy with their bodies,
and that, by age fourteen, half of all girls cite their figures
as their number one worry.[8]

I remember all of this primping, preening and self-
improvement being a lot of fun. Of course it was – this is
how we'd learned to have fun our whole lives short. And
I also remember the affection and supportiveness in those
tweenage bedrooms: how, contrary to so many portrayals of
girls new to double figures, we were full of reassurance and
love for each other. You're not fat; your boobs will grow;
I wish I had your skin; I wish I had your hair; borrow this
skirt – it looks better on you; no one at school hates you; I
think he *does* like you; I promise I won't tell anyone.

Once, at a sleepover, Órla, Lorraine and I gave each other

makeovers, took (what we believed to be) totally stylish pictures (pre-digital, so we had to wait a week to find out they were all profoundly creepy) and wrote each other lists of ten things we liked about each other. I'll always remember the joy of reading my lists, and I'll always be friends with the women who were those girls. In many ways, I'm grateful for our early teenage rites. Makeovers and sleepovers taught me to trust others with my fears and insecurities; they taught me how to listen to the fears and insecurities of others.

This said, I wonder what these rites would look like if they were not centred on grooming? That even the intimacy of female friendship, that bedrock of my adult development, is inextricable from emotions related to socially-sanctioned performances of femininity, is disturbing. It doesn't make the relationships shallow – the bonds we formed are holding strong a decade and a half later – but it does make me wonder how much good we were actually doing each other when five out of the ten items on our loving lists were things like 'has beautiful eyes' or 'has great fashion sense'. This misgiving is cemented when I look at the young adulthoods of those three not-quite-kids: we've all struggled with eating and body issues.

There was a notable difference, of course, between the childhood rehearsals and the early-teen dress run, which was that all of our meddling and muddling with nails and hair and make-up now had a logical purpose: the attraction of boys. Our friends could write us all the lists they liked, but now there was an objective measure of the success of our performances – male attention.

When men say I'm sweet as candy
As around in a dance we whirl,
It goes to my head like brandy,
I enjoy being a girl!

I still believed, though our rites and rituals had become more diverse, our posturing of maleness and femaleness more pronounced, that boys and girls were the same on the inside. As a child I learned that to be proud of being a girl was to be proud of all this 'girly' stuff. Now, I learned that a significant end of all this 'girly' stuff – of striving to be thin and pretty and stylish – was to attract boys.

The unspoken logic was that a very important part of being a girl was being liked by boys. If the 'girls/boys are better than boys/girls' wars had still been ongoing, I'd have realised that the barricades were un-womaned and the ladyfort was surrounded. But I wasn't playing that game anymore! I was too old to pretend not to like boys. And I put a whole lot of effort into making them like me.

When someone with eyes that smoulder
Says he loves ev'ry silken curl
That falls on my iv'ry shoulder,
I enjoy being a girl!

I wouldn't have owned up to recognising male attention as the underlying logic for having pride in my femininity. But, actually, taking all the evidence into account, it was the explanation for enjoying being a girl that made most sense. The values underlying the books, television programmes and films I had been consuming since I was a child were really only comprehensible if boys were in fact better than girls. If this was so, it made sense that male esteem was more valuable than female esteem.

Why did George from *The Famous Five* always proclaim that she was 'as good as any boy'? Because she didn't want to be liked for her looks, or for cooking and washing up, like pretty, subservient, 'girly' Anne. George wanted to be liked and valued for her strength, bravery and intelligence – she was never so happy as when someone mistook her for male. I've read passages by feminist writers who warmly enthuse that George was their childhood role model – a brave, quick-witted, passionate girl character who refused to conform to gender norms.

But George was never an inspiration for me. She thought girls were silly. As a girl, I was insulted. More, George was always trying, yet only ever *almost* succeeding, to keep up with Julian and Dick, who would pull rank when the going got toughest. George's pride would inevitably be hurt when the real boys reminded her that, however convincing her performance, she was, in fact, female, and they were honour-bound to protect her. Poor George – cooler than scaredy-cat Anne, for sure, but that wasn't enough. She was lacking the all-important dangly appendage that would make her as good as Julian or Dick.

I'm sure some of you are thinking – yes, but *The Famous Five* was set in the fifties, and, even though you were only a child, you must have been aware that female roles had moved on. To this I'd say: *kind of*. I might have had the capacity to challenge some of the gender norms present in the fiction I consumed, but the worldview it presented was still influential on my own. I learned a lot about girlhood and boyhood from Enid Blyton and other classic kids' literature. And so did my brothers.

Case in point: one summer in Connemara, where we were annually taken on holidays, the gang (us and our multitudinous cousins) was engaged in a very serious war with the neighbouring Kelly children. Having accumulated an arsenal of pine cones and experimented with less-than-expertly-manufactured catapults to varying degrees of success (what was wrong, after all, with simply *throwing* pine cones?), we decided that we needed a secure base to retreat to should our offensive be overpowered by the locals' rural savagery and superior knowledge of the boggy terrain. A long-disused outhouse with a still-functional and locking door was ideal, and we spent hours divesting it of briars to create our very own Fort Knox. Feat accomplished, we had to democratically decide who would play which role in the upcoming war effort.

Minutes later, I had unceremoniously tendered my resignation to the gang and was inside crying to the grown-ups. 'What's the matter, Emer?' asked Auntie Anne. 'They made me the HOUSE MAID!' I wailed. That's right: the house maid. I continue to blame Enid Blyton.

The 'boys are better than girls' logic of other cultural products I consumed as a child was less in-yer-face than the fifties' ideology of Blyton, but it was there. Heroes, it seemed, were almost always male. As a little one I listened to Ringo Starr narrate so much *Thomas the Tank Engine* on my Fisher-Price tape player that by the time I started school

I was speaking with a distinctly Liverpudlian accent and my teacher asked my mother when we'd returned from the UK. In *Thomas the Tank Engine* there are no girl engines (Emily was only added to the seven-engine-strong 'steam team' in 2003 for the television series, partly in response to accusations of sexism), while the carriages – sweet, dependent Annie and Clarabel – are female.

The television programme that I (and probably most Irish children) watched religiously was called *The Den*. The presenter was male (first Ian Dempsey, then Ray D'Arcy), as were his two awesome puppet sidekicks, Zig and Zag, their puppy Zuppy and the later addition of Dustin the Turkey. Of all the cartoons this masculine conglomerate of flesh and felt offered to my elastic young mind, I can't remember one – not one[*] – that had a female protagonist: not *Teenage Mutant Ninja Turtles*, *Scooby Doo*, *Captain Planet*, *Count Duckula*, *Inspector Gadget*, *Johnny Bravo*, *Rugrats*, nor *Animaniacs*.[†] Research proves my memory correct.

The computer games I played on our Super Nintendo reproduced the pattern: *Mario*, *Donkey Kong*, *Kirby*, *Yoshi*, Link in *Zelda*, everyone except Princess in *Mario Kart*, everyone except Chun Li in *Street Fighter*. To an outsider observing, looking at three children watching cartoons or playing computer games, it might seem that my brothers

---

[*] I can remember programmes for older kids like *The Girl from Tomorrow*, and *Sabrina the Teenage Witch* that had female protagonists, but no cartoons.

[†] Originally all three Warner Brothers characters were conceived of as male, but Dot, the Warner sister, even if added as an afterthought, was pretty darn brilliant. As an aside, remember Hello Nurse? The chesty nurse in a miniskirt who functioned as an object for Wakko and Yakko to perve on? That's a cool thing to be in a children's programme, isn't it?

and I were having similar experiences. But we were not. The boys were learning that they were the protagonists, and I was learning that I was the understudy. Or the house maid.

Looking into *The Den*'s layout and programming now, I can see that things have changed considerably – it is now presented by two humans, one of whom is a woman, and two puppets, one of whom has a high-pitched voice and ribbons adorning its head. There are more female cartoon characters included in its programming too. Go Powerpuff Girls! But let's not get over-excited: cartoons still feature predominantly male lead characters, and there have been a number of studies into the effects of this on children.

In 1995, researchers Eugenia Zerbinus and Teresa Thompson summarised evidence from the seventies onwards showing that female characters are under-represented in cartoons, and that they are typically lower status.[9] While noting modest improvement, they found that the trend continued strongly into the nineties. In 1997 they asked: 'Do children notice that boys predominate in cartoons and that characters are often stereotyped?' The answer was yes for a majority of the children surveyed, and, significantly, the researchers found that children who noticed gender-stereotypic behaviours in cartoon characters reported more traditional job expectations for themselves and for others.[10] Indeed, there's a strong body of evidence indicating that children's TV viewing is positively correlated with their degree of gender stereotyping. This, I'd argue, indicates that children can recognise gender stereotypes in the products they consume, but lack the capacity to question and critically evaluate them.

In 2002 a research team analysed the degree of gender stereotyping across different genres of cartoons, and found that lessons children were likely to learn about gender from watching cartoons include the idea that men are more important than women, the idea that men are aggressive and get into fights, and the idea that women are fearful or nurturing.[11] A study from 2012 found that television exposure was significantly related to children's self-esteem, and that watching TV decreased the confidence of all children of colour and all female children, while it increased the self-esteem of white, male children.[12]

As we get older and start consuming adult cultural products, the pattern doesn't change. The graphic novelist Alison Bechdel once drew a strip called 'The Rule', which became quite famous. In it, two women are trying to figure out what to see at the cinema, and one tells the other that she has a rule: she'll only go to see films in which there are at least two female characters, who actually talk to each other, about something other than a man. This has come to be known as the Bechdel test. According to Bechdeltest. com, only 54 per cent of films pass this ludicrously simple feminist exam, and many do so dubiously, because the women talk to each other briefly, or about babies, marriage or equally stereotypically-feminine fare.

It's not just television and film either. If you're bookish, like me, you learn early on that great literature is largely the preserve of men. Reading the classics means filling your head with male voices: male voices that create female characters. And these female characters become part of you, of your understanding of how to perform womanhood. There are exceptions obviously – George Eliot was secretly not George at all, and, of course, there's Austen and the Brontës, but the bulk of canonical literature is by white men.

The Kenyan writer Ngũgĩ Wā Thiong'o talks about growing up in colonial Africa and having a European education. When we think about European colonialism, we tend to think about Europeans colonizing people's lands and resources – dispossessing them of material things. But Wā Thiong'o talks about how his *mind* was colonised by his education: how, constantly, he encountered images of bestial, inhuman Africans in the 'civilised' and 'superior' European literature and philosophy that he studied at school and university. He internalised these images – his understanding of the world was based on tacit, unspoken acceptance of his own inferiority. Africa might have won its independence, but, for Wā Thiong'o, decolonising African minds is the ongoing struggle.[13]

Women's minds are also colonised. In a huge proportion of the cultural products that we consume at home and in school, from Shakespeare to Spiderman, women are decorative and domestic – the warm-up number, but rarely the headline act.

While my parents and teachers might have told me that girls and boys were equal, life taught me differently: that boys were the main characters – the Thomas the Tank Engines; and girls were the sidekicks – the Annies and Clarabels. This difference in the way girls and boys are valued was embedded in my worldview and, as the studies on children, gender and TV I discuss above suggest, as a child I probably didn't have the faculties to break down the prejudiced views I was consuming. So can there be any more natural thing, if you're a girl, than to subconsciously start to look to men for validation, by performing the actions and speaking the lines that you think will make men like you?

When I hear the compliment'ry whistle
That greets my bikini by the sea,
I turn and I glower and I bristle,
But I'm happy to know the whistle's meant for me!

I couldn't be a boy, and, unlike Enid Blyton's George, I didn't want to be. So the next best thing was for boys to like me. And for boys to like me I needed to be considered attractive. I mean, I was hardly going to impress men through my in-depth knowledge of the life cycle of the Liver Fluke (Latin: *Fasciola hepatica*), now was I? Nor with my 'game' of finding ways to do theorems that weren't in the maths book. I had yet to see a boy go wild when he asked to cog my geography homework and witnessed my meticulously rendered stage-by-stage diagrams of sea-stack formation. Even my extracurricular activities in the choir and school musicals, which should have been at least *kind of* sexy, only seemed to add to my overall aura of nerd. I always considered being bookish to be an inconvenient genetic flaw. I was Cuthbert the class swot, when I so badly wanted to be any other Bash Street Kid (Toots, probably, as she was the only female Bash Street Kid).

So, obviously, I wasn't going to get any male attention in school. I didn't have the right tracksuit bottoms, and I put way too much expression into my voice when I was asked to read poetry in English. I focused my energies on boys from other schools who had no way to know that I enjoyed French translation exercises. I acquired army jackets and Nine Inch Nail CDs to fool people into mistaking drastically unhip for 'alternative', and my skirts got shorter, my T-shirts tighter, my hair lighter, my face more painted and my limbs thinner.

Seeing as so much of my social preparation for woman-hood had been focused on my appearance, it was a logical extension to move from pretty to sexy. And, seeing as the positive attention I was used to receiving had been based on my appearance since I was a little girl, it's unsurprising that this was the positive attention that I continued to crave. But something was *different*.

In 2012, I went to see the Iranian-British Comedian Shappi Khorsandi at London's Soho Theatre, and she played out (in comedy that was borderline unbearable to watch but made me laugh 'til everything hurt all the same) the change that her relationship with her father's male friends underwent when she was about fourteen. They went from chucking her under the chin, hoisting her onto their shoulders and spinning her round by the legs to fearfully hugging her for nanoseconds, before looking anywhere – *anywhere* – except at her suddenly sexual, suddenly terrifying teenage skin.

I can't say that, like Khorsandi, I noticed my parents' friends sexualising me at that age. But what I do remember – and maybe this is the difference between growing up in the UK like Khorsandi and growing up in Catholic Ireland like me – is that grown-ups became disapproving of the physical attention I received. I went from being allowed to wear whatever I wanted really – short shorts, crop tops – to being subtly monitored. I remember once, on holiday, age fourteen, coming down to the lobby of a hotel dressed in my friend's brother's thigh-high sports socks and a mini skirt (which my friend Leah and I had decided was a totally winning combo). My parents got really angry.

Looking back, I'm pretty sure they saw adult men looking at me. My mum tried to couch her explanations as to why I had to change in the ridiculousness of wearing sports socks when not actually playing sports, and a dislike for the skirt I'd borrowed from a friend for the holiday. But I'd been allowed to wear the skirt before, with nothing but flip-flops, so I wasn't biting.

Something similar happened again a few months later, when, visiting family in Wales, I wanted to wear animal-print tights and a black miniskirt to Easter mass. My mum got really mad and made me change. Again, it was weird. I'd been allowed to wear the same outfit to mass in Ireland about a year before.

The problem wasn't my clothes (although, admittedly, wearing sports socks when you're not actually playing sports is odd). The problem was that the attention I was receiving now contained a sexual element. Suddenly, strangers' interest in my performance of femininity carried an element of shame – I would get into trouble if I dressed to encourage it – and also, of course, excitement: because what was this new sexual attention if not the biggest and best kind of compliment?

Compliments centred on my appearance had been de rigueur since I was a child. These compliments had only been a good thing before. Clothes and make-up were part of my childhood play and my tweenage rehearsals of womanhood; now that I was almost grown up, a significant part of my energies focused on my appearance. Teen magazines advised me on how to attract men, while books, TV, films and other cultural products subtly reinforced a narrative of male superiority, which was confirmed by the gendered make-up of the world around me. Surely male attention was a good thing? Now I was getting stares, comments and whistles. I didn't glower or bristle at all. I smiled and waved. I liked it! My entire life – toys, cartoons, films, books, friendships – had conditioned me to like it. How could I *not* like it?

I'm strictly a female female
And my future I hope will be
In the home of a brave and free male
Who'll enjoy being a guy having a girl… like… me.

Let's return to Our Mother of Mercy school hall, 1994, to where a troupe of expertly choreographed but poorly coordinated mini-Galwegians is flouncing across the stage, enthusiastically vociferating its enjoyment of the trappings of femininity. The auditorium looks on, deeming the performance harmless, drawing no correlation between the stereotypes of womanhood that these little girls have been taught to ironically enact and the social roles that they will one day be expected to play. The sexism of the performance is an inoffensive joke.

All the world is this stage. The little girls have learned

their lines as directed; their actions have been choreographed and directed by adults, and performing their parts will gain them applause. They're too young to recognise the troubling values present in the songs they are told to sing. By the time they are young women, this song, this routine, has become – like the abilities to count, read or communicate – second nature. Rehearsals are over – it's time for the show!

CHAPTER TWO:

PERFORMING

'In effect the individual is understood in terms of a pre-social essence, nature, or identity and on that basis s/he is invested with a quasi-spiritual autonomy. The individual becomes the origin and focus of meaning – an individuated essence which precedes and – in idealist philosophy – transcends history and society.'

Jonathan Dollimore[14]

THE PRINCESS OF THE PATRIARCHY

I'm eighteen, and I'm very definitely not a feminist. I work full time in a country pub and, after hours, I sit up at the counter with my co-workers and the few faithful punters favoured with a lock-in, drinking gin and slimline tonics paid for by the contents of the tip jar. Feminism is not exactly the primary 2 a.m. topic of conversation in rural West of Ireland, 2003, but one night it rears its hydra heads.

'The problem,' the owner of the pub announces, 'is that women don't want to stay home anymore. They want their own careers.' There are general murmurs of agreement from the mostly-male assembly, affirming that the main cause of social upheaval in modern Ireland is the lack of women willing to have a hot dinner on the table for their hardworking menfolk of an evening.

One of the night's hangers-on is a musician, perhaps in her early thirties, and she says, 'but my career is important to me.' She is lambasted with questions like 'who's supposed to take care of the kids?' When she suggests that childcare and domestic tasks could be shared, she's told it's not practical to share, and that women are better able for kids and housework. Isn't that the way it's always been? Isn't it natural? She backs off, saying it's for individuals to decide. 'What do you think, Emer?' asks the owner, my boss.

And with a flick of my expensively highlighted hair and a flutter of my heavily mascara'd lashes, I become Jesus amongst the wise men in the temple, holding them rapt with the sagacity of my scriptures. 'I'd quite like to stay home when I have kids, actually. It'd be lovely. You'd get to play with the little ones all day – you wouldn't have to go out to work or anything. Women are lucky, because men don't have that option really. I can't wait to be a mum.' I can feel the warm glow of approval enveloping me. 'Jayz, there's still a few good ones left, hah?' contributes Willy from his barstool.

Encouraged, I continue. 'Do ye know, I think lots of women play victim, instead of looking at all the wonderful things about being a woman. So they'll say "isn't it terrible that women have to take their husband's names when they get married", but I think that's a really beautiful, generous thing to do. I'd definitely take my husband's name.' I have the pub in my steam-chapped palm. 'And it's the same – giving out about staying at home. Isn't it a nice option to have? There are all sorts of great things about being a girl that men don't get to experience, like getting dressed up for a night out. I often think – are ye not jealous?' This elicits some laughter and something about the pleasure being in the looking. This, in turn, leads to a lament that some women do be fierce cross if they catch you looking. Eyes turn to me once more for my holy pronouncements on checking out and chatting up.

'Ah now, those girls complaining about a few arse-pats and wolf-whistles, they're awful whiners – won't they miss it when it's gone?' Oh-ho, they will, they will, they will, rumbles my Greek chorus. 'I like a bit of attention. Sure, what's the point of all the pain that goes into beauty if it's not appreciated? Enjoy it, I think! Isn't it a compliment?' Oh-ho, it is, it is, it is.

At this point, the musician chimes back in. 'I'm not a feminist,' she says, 'but I think you'll feel different when you're older – when you've experienced more, when you've seen that the world isn't always an equal place.' I am eighteen, and I know everything, so I'm quick to voice my worldly scorn. 'I've never experienced *any* discrimination. Ever. It's not 1950! Sexism doesn't exist anymore. I've always been treated the same as the lads – at school, at work. Everyone knows that men and women are equal now.'

The musician is a soft and un-argumentative soul, but I seemed to have stirred her to enough passion for something resembling a challenge to my barstool throne. 'How would you explain,' she asks, 'the fact that the vast majority of people in positions of power – the people at the top of almost every industry – are men? Is it because they're the hardest workers, or the most talented, or the most intelligent? How would you explain it?'

This might have stumped me, if it had not been for the aforementioned fact of my omniscience. 'Women *choose* to stay home with their children. No one's forcing them! They have the right to go out to work. It's their choice.'

And there we have it – choice. The reason for the lack of women in positions of power, the reason women spend so much time, money and mental energy on how they look, the reason they take their husbands' names, the reason they bear the brunt of domestic labour and childcare – all of these things are *choices*.

As feminists, we shouldn't judge other women's choices. But we should very certainly try to understand women's choices. And understanding choice in a meaningful way means looking beyond the individual to society. We are not born wanting fake breasts or a work-life based on unpaid domestic labour any more than we are born wanting a can of Coke or Nike runners. In significant ways, society creates our desires and expectations for ourselves. Yet we are also individuals, capable of acting in accordance with or contrary to societal expectations. So in what sense are our choices really our choices?

STRUCTURE AND AGENCY

We're talking about what's known in sociology as the tension between structure and agency. Agency refers to the individual – to the choices she makes. Structure refers to society – to the context that produced the individual, and in which she continues to act. Which of these factors most determines the person I am and the behaviours I perform? Obviously, this question is impossible to answer absolutely, and so the debate over structure and agency is nuanced, deep, and – for me at least – endlessly fascinating.[15]

The first important thing to know about the structure and agency debate is that it is political. If you believe evangelically in agency – that the individual is entirely free to choose whatever she wants to do – then you're unlikely to see the social factors that influence a person's actions. This means that you're more likely to blame disadvantaged people for their problems, believing any misfortune to be the result of choices they've made. You're also more likely to believe that advantaged people choose to work hard and thus deserve their goodies. Conservative and capitalist worldviews tend to privilege agency in their explanations for an individual's actions.

So, for example, if you believe in the primacy of agency, you might see a teenager stealing a pair of Nikes from a high-street shop and think, 'what a morally bankrupt little criminal, taking what does not belong to her!' You might completely ignore the fact that most petty criminals come from impoverished backgrounds, or that they live in a society with a big gap between rich and poor, where they constantly receive the message from media and advertising that branded clothing will make them more valuable. You might see no difference between this girl stealing a pair of shoes that she can't afford and a well-paid politician stealing taxpayers' money by putting luxury items on his expense account.

Or, if you believe in the primacy of agency, you might see a single mother on benefits and think, 'things might be challenging for her, sure, but she's made her bed.' You might ignore the fact that the woman comes from an economically disadvantaged area, went to an overstretched and under-funded school, and thus lacks qualifications; you mightn't stop to consider that in a country with high childcare costs, which isn't geared towards flexible working hours for parents, it's very difficult – emotionally and practically – for a single mother to get a job. You might see no difference between this woman using social welfare to survive and an Oxford graduate going on the dole for a year so that she can party with her mates in London.

On the other hand, if you believe devoutly in structure – that an individual's actions are always the product of her social situation – you can fail to recognise and honour people's achievements. Overall, liberal and socialist world-views tend to privilege structure in their explanations for an individual's actions.

Thinking about agency is important. People brought up in similar situations can become very different people: the sister of the Nike-thieving teenager, for example, may never have stolen anything in her life. Maybe she studied like crazy and, against the odds, became a doctor. Who in their right mind would say that structure as opposed to agency is responsible for her nice car and her nice house? In short, some people work very hard for their advantages. Focusing on structure can disregard the experiences of people who don't fit the statistics, and those people's experiences are important too.

Some people (for the record: not me) believe that focusing on structure absolves the individual of responsibility. So, for example, they'd say that in focusing on the background of single mothers on benefits, we're saying that these women don't have a responsibility towards their own fertility or employment prospects. (The reason I think this is a weak critique is that it's very obviously much easier for some people to be 'responsible' than others.)

All but the most blindly zealous acknowledge that, when explaining human behaviour, we need to look at both structure *and* agency. If you focus too hard on agency, you don't see the big picture. If you focus too hard on structure, you don't see the exceptions to the rule.

In our media culture, agency is often used to fob people off when they try to look at structural problems. Remember the London riots of 2011? Politicians and the press painted the rioters as opportunistic, psychopathic, greedy little thugs, hungry for a new pair of sneakers. The media seized on the (very few) middle-class people participating in the riots, and no official inquiry into the underlying cause of the rioting was commissioned. This is in spite of the fact that, during the Thatcher years, a report into similar riots found that those involved suffered from racial discrimination and economic deprivation, and recommended urgently investing money in the affected areas.[16]

Similarly, the press regularly lambasts 'lazy' single mothers, whom they claim choose to have babies in order to get free houses and money and diamonds and sports cars. This agency-based logic is very powerful. It's justification for the constant assault on the incomes of vulnerable people:

a 2011 report from the Institute of Fiscal Studies showed that single mothers were disproportionately disadvantaged by government spending policy, and could expect to lose 8.5 per cent of their total income by 2015.[17]

It's easier to point a finger at a teenager caught red-handed or a mum on benefits than it is to examine an entire system. And the public responds better to stories that hinge on agency. A human face makes something seem real, while ideas as abstract as economics or culture are harder to emotionally engage with.

I've pointed out that agency-based logic is closely related with capitalism and structure-based logic more so with socialism: now I'd like to tease this out a little. We live in a society that is based largely on capitalism, and partly on socialism. Capitalism is the idea that individuals own things – like property, goods, ideas, logos and animals (not other people anymore, thankfully) – and capitalism is driven by individual profit. Socialism is the idea that people should collectively own these same things – and it's driven by what's best for society overall.

A capitalist society is one in which everyone is trying to make money from the things they own (if only from their own bodies). In the purest capitalist system, if you stop making money and no one voluntarily helps you, you drop out of society: if you can't afford to eat, then you will die. In our system, we tax everyone and distribute some of the money to those in need so that this doesn't happen. That's a socialist element.

So why is capitalism all about agency? Why does capitalism like the logic of choice? Well, because capitalism *needs* choice. It's a very unequal system, in which the richest 1 per cent of the planet own 40 per cent of the entire world's wealth, while the poorest 50 per cent own only 1 per cent between them.[18] That's globally, but within individual societies there are also massive gaps between the haves and the have-nots. In the UK the richest 1 per cent own 10 per cent of the wealth and the poorest 50 per cent share 18 per cent between them.[19] In the US, the richest 1 per cent own 35 per cent of the wealth and the poorest 50 per cent share 1.1 per cent between them.[20] And the people at the bottom and the people at the top are not a random jumble of demographics: white men rule the roost; women have less; people of colour have less; people who were born poor, stay poor. (We must never forget, of course, that there are individual exceptions to these patterns.)

Capitalism needs choice, because, if people choose their inequality, then capitalism is not unfair. Look at the kinds of success stories our culture likes to tell us: some talented people choose to work hard, and they end up with the power and the money. It's a meritocracy. Anyone can go from rags to riches – all they need is talent, drive and a little sprinkling of good luck. From Julia Roberts in *Pretty Woman*, to Will Smith in *The Pursuit of Happyness*, to the latest winner of *The X Factor*, our culture tells us that the capitalist dream is a reality – anyone can make it if they try.

This logic is endemic to how people think about gender issues. For example, rather than looking at women leaving work in their droves after childbirth and seeing a social structure that doesn't adequately provide for the fact that 50 per cent of people exist in bodies that produce future humans, we see people who exist in bodies that produce future humans *choosing* to bow out of the workforce. Or, rather than looking at the 'beauty' industry as symptomatic of a structure that profits from teaching women to hate their bodies, we see women *choosing* faddy diet plans, botox injections, liposuction and laser hair removal. Instead of looking at obstacles to women's representation in positions of power, we see women *choosing* to stay out of politics. Instead of looking at a society that places more value on men's narratives than women's narratives and trivialises domestic violence, we see abused women foolishly *choosing* to stay in violent relationships.

To explain human behaviour, we need to think about both structure and agency. But focusing solely on agency – on choice – means ignoring disadvantage. This blindness is good for those who are already privileged – whether it is by gender, sexuality, race, class or ability – but it's bad for equality, and very certainly bad for women.

WHOSE LINES ARE THESE ANYWAY?

Let's take what we know about structure and agency and return to Galway 2003, where we left an 18-year-old anti-feminist downing low-cal G&Ts and telling the pub exactly what it wanted to hear. Clearly, I was gaining praise and prestige within a sexist system by espousing sexist values myself. I didn't know I was doing this, of course. I'd spent my life learning how to perform the version of femininity my society expected – I'd been socialised and conditioned into beliefs and behaviours which I accepted as common sense without really examining them. I was skilled at the performance and, in some ways, I enjoyed it.

But in some ways I didn't. I hated being grabbed by men when I went out to nightclubs. Once, in fact, when a man continued to put his hand up my skirt and grab my vagina in spite of being politely and impolitely requested not to do so, I turned sweetly, asked him for a drag of his cigarette, and stubbed the butt out on his face (a fact of which I am not proud).

I was veering close to dangerously underweight again, I had no periods, and my relationship with food and my body was daily psychological torture. It had probably been a year since I'd left the house without make-up. With a good leaving certificate in my back pocket, I had dropped out of my science degree at university and was sitting around trying to impress a bunch of drunken auld fellas with a performance of perfectly presented, delightfully domesticated, comely, compliant femininity.

What did the structure in which I exercised my agency look like? I came from a home in which my working mother did all of the housework and cooking. I tried to help with this work, while my brothers, in the main, did not. When I asked them to help, they treated me as though I was a nag. I watched my mother work from 7 a.m. 'til 9 p.m. or later almost every day, and this shaped both my sense of responsibility towards domestic tasks and my expectations for combining work and family.

Sadly, my experience is in no way unique. Women's increased participation in the labour force hasn't meant a proportionate decrease in their unpaid domestic labour. Simply put: working women have two jobs. According to the Institute for Public Policy Research, based on statistics collected in the UK in 2013, married women of working age still do approximately three times the domestic work of their partners, excluding childcare, for which women are also significantly more responsible.[21] In the US, when a heterosexual couple both work full time, the woman does about 40 per cent more childcare and 30 per cent more housework than the man.[22]

What was I supposed to do about this? If I stopped helping at home, my mother was left with all the unpaid domestic labour. If I'd kept doing it, I upheld the unequal system. If I tried to get my brothers or father to help, I was met with ridicule and negativity. The men I loved liked me less if I asked to be treated as an equal. I'd been conditioned to desire male approval – so this was painful. It was too hard to confront the social structure I was both trapped in and reinforcing. It was too easy for the men in my family to pretend they didn't see it. So I helped, and I said that it was not because I was a girl, but because it was my choice.

I had a heavily made-up face, shaved legs, expensive hair, tight clothing and an underweight body. I knew, instinctively, to hide my book smarts at work. I grew up in a media culture where men needed to be talented to succeed, whereas women needed to be pretty. A focus on my appearance marked my childhood out as different from that of my brothers, and taught me the importance of look-ing and acting girly, as had my toys, cartoons, my teen magazines, TV shows, films and the weekly 'thinspiration' of the *Sunday Times Style* magazine. It seems incredible that I explained my guilty striving for the perfect body in terms of choice, yet I did.

I was obviously desperate to impress the men around me. Why did I want their approval so badly? Perhaps because boys were the most important characters in the cartoons I watched as a child, and the creators of the majority of books and films that I consumed as a young adult. By the time I'd read my way through the works of my (then) favourite authors, Dostoyevsky, Kerouac and Orwell – all male writers whom my culture had taught me were very important indeed – I'd subconsciously internalised a belief in male superiority.

My un-confronted belief that men were superior made me look for male attention. This meant saying and doing things of which men would approve. Because within a sexist society one way that we, as women, can gain power is to take on sexist values ourselves.

As this book probably testifies, I eventually came to see that putting all my chips on choice was a losing gamble. I became aware of the larger social structures that influenced my thoughts and actions. It took over a decade, but I learned to refuse the kind of happiness to be derived from inferior social status but very pretty shoes, and demand more of myself and of the world. Over the next ten years, I started to play with performing differently, and came to see my past behaviours not as choices, but as an act for which I'd spent my life rehearsing. And I was, in equal parts, embarrassed and angry when I found that my anti-feminist attitudes were not reasonable individual opinions at all, but the spoken lines most useful to the patriarchy.

CHAPTER THREE:

PLAYING DRESS-UP

'We're born naked, and the rest is drag.'

RuPaul

TRICK OR TREAT

Halloween. Glorious, grotesque Halloween. It's a holiday especially for theatre luvvies: the feast day of St Drama Queen. As a kid, I'd go wild. I'd have my friends rehearsing trick or treat routines for weeks in advance. And we're not talking your run-of-the-mill 'Smell my feet, Give me something good to eat' rigamarole. We're talking coordinated costumes. We're talking characters. Our rhymes were all original compositions (by whom, I'll leave you to guess); our choreography may have been simple (I wasn't working with professionals), but, sweet Lord, was it precise.

I've always loved Halloween, and not just because it allowed me to coax my cast, sorry, my *friends*, into a gruelling rehearsal schedule with the promise of earning more sweets than they could stuff their greedy little faces with in a lifetime (strangely, no one ever objected that the other neighbourhood children also got sweets, regardless of the synchronicity of

51

their broomstick manoeuvres). I've always loved Halloween because it's a time when normal rules don't apply.

It's late, it's dark – yet children roam the streets. Usually encouraged to be good, on this one night they can behave like little monsters. They can knock on adults' doors and demand hyperactivity-inducing confectioneries; if refused, they are socially entitled to throw eggs at adults' windows. Everyone is dressed as whatever fiendish thing they like, revelling in the anonymity of being masked. Halloween is beautiful bedlam: it's carnival.

Mikhail Bakhtin was a Russian thinker who described something that happens in literature, and sometimes in life, that he called the Carnivalesque. The Carnivalesque is a time when normal rules and hierarchies get turned on their heads. It's a time of humour – a time for poking fun at power. Beggars become kings; the wise become fools; angels become devils; women become men; children become adults; prisoners become gaolers. While the Carnivalesque lasts, people are free to interact with each other however they choose. No social decorum is required. There are no strangers from whom to keep a distance. In the world of the Carnivalesque, everyone is strange.[23]

You look around. People you thought you knew are acting out of character. People you don't recognise are doing things you'd never expect to see – flapping in fountains, dancing in graveyards. And all of these strangest of strangers know that they can act without consequence. Just for this one day, this one night, this Carnivalesque time, nobody is going to call the gentlefolk in white coats, nor the less than gentle folk in blue uniforms. And so, things that are usually kept separate unite, things usually considered sacred are laughed at, and, together, a society colludes to create something almost its opposite – something spontaneous, unpredictable, even dangerous. Then, the very next morning, everyone goes back to the same old routine, just like nothing ever happened.

This whole idea has always made me think – why *does* a society go back to normal after a Carnivalesque time? When they've seen their king begging and their priest sinning, and they know the day-to-day binaries and hierarchies are arbitrary and artificial, how can they go back to the same old drudge? Halloween annually freed me from my girl-child coded clothing, and into skeleton costumes and zombie masks. Okay, so I was more likely to be a witch than my brothers, but overall, it was a time when being sweet and girly was definitely not required. Why, the next day, didn't I demand to wear my ketchup-soaked bandages to school? Fear of consequence?

Thinking beyond Halloween, there are events in most of our lives that make us look at facts about society that we've always taken for granted – that we've always believed are common sense, perhaps, or that we've just never taken the time to question – and think: wait a second, there's no good reason things should be this way. There are times when we realise that everyone is behaving in certain patterns out of convention rather than out of necessity, and that the ways they're behaving are, when you look for logic, inexplicable. But it's rare that we follow through on these realisations by changing our routines and our habits. Why? Fear of what the neighbours might say? Or because it's hard to imagine new ways to act?

SCARIER THAN GHOSTS

I reached an age where, unlike Lindsay Lohan in *Mean Girls*, I got the memo that Halloween costumes should be sexy not scary. At fourteen, I discovered the word 'diaphanous' and built an ensemble around it, aiming for a bramble-torn, woodland nymph aesthetic. The wings were ripped neck scarves that my mother never wore and probably didn't want anyway. I half-sellotaped and (ill-advisedly) half-superglued ivy to my calves and thighs, and painstakingly painted trellises of leaves and flowers along my clavicle and around my midriff.

I was a rather scantily clad fairy, and not, it must be admitted, particularly petrifying. Costume complete, I realised I'd forgotten to get the flagon of cider I'd stashed in the field, and had to flutter over the wall and through the long grass to recover the forbidden nectar. Ever the method actor, me.

Age fifteen, I donned a totally culturally sensitive Geisha costume. Nothing says undead like traditional Japanese entertainer, especially if you add stilettos and fishnets and ensure that your dress has a split up to the arse.

Age sixteen, I went for a chic underage fetish club look with a French maid costume. I'd finally discovered the kind of translation exercise that did impress the boys!

Age seventeen, a dominatrix police woman took control of scare-town, with a baby pink PVC hat and Spice Girl-inspired fuck-me boots rescued from the back of the wardrobe.

Age eighteen, I was a hula dancer – an outfit singularly suited to a West of Ireland late-October night. Not.

And age nineteen? Age nineteen, something different happened. I strapped my breasts down with a scarf, put on a pair of Ciarán's X-Worx trousers, a baggy t-shirt, a pair of Ronan's shoes with socks stuffed in the toes, covered my blondie mane with a Liverpool FC beanie hat and gave myself chin shadow and extra eyebrow with black eyeliner. I lowered my voice and changed my gait. I was a boy. Pretty lo-fi Halloween effort, really. But a convincing one.

I don't know precisely why I decided to leave X-rated raunch behind for the year. I guess I thought a boy costume might be fun. But I also suspect that a feminist conscious-ness was – sleepily, yawning and grumbling – beginning to emerge. I was starting to question the rhetoric of individual merit and choice that had been the bedrock of my ideas about gender.

I'd gone back to university and was studying psychology, philosophy, French and English. It was such an exciting time – I was being given tools to think about society, politics, culture and what it means to exist at all; I was surrounded by people who wanted to talk about this stuff as much as I did; my brain was going 'ping' all day long; and – at very long last – it was cool to be bookish.

But my all-encompassing nerd joy also brought me to some unpleasant realisations about society and about myself. If men and women were equal, why were the vast majority of texts I was studying written by men? Okay, the canon of ancient or classic philosophy was composed of mostly male voices for an obvious reason: the millennia-long oppression of women. However, my courses on contemporary philosophy had hardly any female thinkers on the syllabus either, and we studied far more male than female authors, poets and playwrights in my literature classes, too. Something didn't add up.

It was hard, too, learning how to think from philosophers who believed that women couldn't think. Aristotle was a big influence on my conception of ethics, but I had to absorb his sexism alongside his wisdom. This wasn't really problematised: I was just supposed to shrug it off. Similarly, when I studied the early-nineteenth-century philosopher Hegel, I was both inspired and insulted.

Hegel believed that what he called reciprocal recognition was fundamental to the human spirit.[24] So, in order to be fulfilled as a human being – to value yourself and the world – you have to be recognised by another person. What Hegel means by 'recognised' is disputed, but I think it's useful to think of it as 'understood and respected as an equal'. Your recognition can't come from just any other person. It can't be a person whom you don't respect, or whom you see as only instrumental to your desires and ambitions. It has to be a person whom you yourself recognise.

In hindsight, this is extremely relevant to feminism, because in our society many men don't respect women as equals and many women see men as obstacles to their desires and ambitions. If we were to apply Hegelian theory, this situation means that a cycle of power struggles will continue until women and men recognise each other. But in Hegelian philosophy the superiority of men is just taken as given: he says that a woman's greatest vocation and ambition is marriage, because in marriage she gets the recognition she needs from her husband. However, because the recognition a woman gives cannot be equal to a man's, men must get recognition from other men. For Hegel, women are like plants – passive – and men like animals – active.*

Again, I was supposed to shrug this off. I was learning the very concepts that were shaping my understanding of meaningful human existence from someone who thought that women didn't have meaningful human existences. And, despite this pretty major flaw in his ability to perceive the human world – i.e. thinking that half of humanity is intellectually inferior – Hegel was held up as an authoritative source of wisdom on the human condition.

Maybe ignoring this was easy for the male lecturer, who was absorbing the idea that this great thinker, like so many great thinkers, believed members of his sex superior to members of my sex, but it affected my confidence in my intellectual abilities. Of course it did. It's just that I didn't realise it was affecting my confidence.

---

* Here's Hegel in his own words *ahem*: 'Women are capable of education, but they are not made for activities which demand a universal faculty such as the more advanced sciences, philosophy and certain forms of artistic production. Women may have happy ideas, taste and elegance, but they cannot attain to the ideal. The difference between men and women is like that between animals and plants. Men correspond to animals, while women correspond to plants because their development is more placid and the principle that underlies it is the rather vague unity of feeling. When women hold the helm of government, the state is at once in jeopardy, because women regulate their actions not by the demands of universality but by arbitrary inclinations and opinions. Women are educated – who knows how? – as it were by breathing in ideas, by living rather than by acquiring knowledge. The status of manhood, on the other hand, is attained only by the stress of thought and much technical exertion.' Hegel, *Philosophy of Right*, 1820. (Available free electronically from numerous online sources.)

Then one day I was reading a text by one of the rare female philosophers on my syllabus – Hannah Arendt – and I became aware that the way I was reading it was different. I was interacting with it much more critically, challenging her ideas as I went along, holding them up to the light to look for cracks. It dawned on me that when reading male philosophers, I would often accept what they said rather than working through my objections thoroughly. I presumed that the great white male minds had already considered and dealt with my counter-arguments in ways that I wasn't yet advanced enough to predict. But with Arendt I wasn't accepting anything she said without having explored all alternative avenues. I realised that I was doing this because I thought I was capable of being the intellectual equal of this female philosopher. I realised that I myself was sexist. I'll never forget that moment.

In *Feminism is for Everybody*, Bell Hooks explains that women can't band together to fight inequality before they first confront their own sexist thinking, as well as the ways in which some women oppress others because of sexuality, race or class.[25] For me, the experience of my own sexist prejudice was what got me thinking seriously about equality in the first place. Awareness of my other biases began to follow.

Perhaps I'm equating the first playful desires to start experimenting with the gendered status quo too closely with this awakening, but it's the best answer I have for why I started wanting to perform differently. There are probably other reasons – my love of the dramatic, of dress-up, of theatre – yet, looking back, it feels as though experimenting with gender norms, however light-heartedly at first, was part of my new obsession with questioning power structures in the world around me.

The boy Halloween costume was remarkably effective. Maybe it's because I have quite an angular jaw and am not particularly curvy. Maybe it's because I did a lot of acting, and was able to keep in character. Maybe it's because no one expected me to be out for Halloween dressed as anything other than a pole-dancing sex zombie. But almost definitely, as we'll discuss later in this chapter, it was also for deeper reasons of culture, perception and psychology.

At any rate, as an über-femme, looks-obsessed young woman hits the town on Halloween night to join the Galway ghouls, wearing nothing more scary than her little brother's trousers, this book departs from the social and cultural processes that teach us to perform girly behaviours and internalise sexist beliefs. It becomes about change: about performing differently, about trying to rewrite the script, about breaking down the conditioning that makes us into stereotypically gendered people.

But enough chit-chat – it's Halloween night. Let's party with the boys!

ACCIDENTAL EXPERIMENTS IN PERFORMING GENDER

(Note – the tone here is based on my nineteen-year-old blog. I genuinely used to talk like this. And write like this. I have provided footnotes for some of the more challenging Galway vocabulary. I'm also considering providing an apology to anyone who used to hang out with me when I was nineteen, but, on reflection, I'm pretty sure they talked like this too.)

I don't know what made me to decide to be a fien* for Halloween, really. I figured it'd be fun. More fun than trying to be the sexiest skank in Galway awenaise.† I didn't expect to learn anything. But then I did learn stuff, which is deadly.‡ Halloween is baloobas,§ and everyone expects things to be off, so I wonder if I tried to be a boy on some other night, if the reactions I got wouldn't be more aggressive, if my actions wouldn't have more consequence. But hey, you got to start somewhere, and Halloween is where I'm starting.

I rock up to The Warwick Hotel for Strange Brew, the deadliest¶ club night in Galvegas.** I see my heads†† at a table by the dancefloor, so I grab a pint of the black shtuff,‡‡ and mosey mannishly on over. I'm hyper-aware of my gait, of trying to stay grounded, masculine, heavy. I remember, once, me and Ronan sitting on the wall outside our gaf,§§ watching a neighbour who'd turned twelve and started secondary school on his way home. 'When did he start walking like that?' I said, following the newly-adopted, slightly-lopsided

---

* Boy
† Anyways
‡ Cool
§ Crazy. This word has a really awful etymology and I don't use it anymore. But I didn't know that when I was nineteen.
¶ Coolest
** Exactly like Las Vegas, except a small, rainy city with cobbled streets. Oh. Wait.
†† People
‡‡ Guinness
§§ House

swagger with my eyes. 'Sure, he's been practising all summer in front of the mirror,' said Ronan. And we had a giggle, because the funniest stuff is true. And that's what it's like for me now – my walk is something conscious, something I need to practise with the world as my mirror. I construct the shape of my shoulders. I adopt a nonchalant, slow, skater-ish step, trying to channel my first boyfriend Dave, who was as slight as me and not much taller, but always oozed boyish trouble.

I approach the table, and my friends look up as if to say, 'who the funk?' They're expecting Emer, you see, and they've probably been taking bets as to what pornographic version of a mythological yoke* she'll arrive barely dressed as this year. 'Hi lads,' I say in my huskiest tenor. 'Hi,' reply one or two, looking confused. My friend Michelle's boyfriend, currently Oberon to her Titania, is the first to deck. 'No way!' he says. 'What?' says Michelle. 'Look at the eyes, like,' he answers. 'Feck off!' says Shell, 'that's amazing.' My Galwegians budge on over, and I sit down to drink amid the painted crew, who are stunned they could be so easily fooled.

It's tempting to break character in the company of my oldies but goodies, but I keep it unreal. I remember to make my voice low, keep my shoulders square. When I find myself reaching to lick the Guinness froth from my cupid's bow with the tip of my tongue, I pause, then suck it on down with my bottom lip, all testosterone. Everything – the way I drink, the way I sit, the way I move my hands, the distance I put between myself and others – is conscious

---

* Thing

and performed. But it's really natural at the same time, as if, from observing the other half of humanity, I've always known how to play the part of boy.

One of my Oran* beures,† Lorraine, arrives, cloaked and devil-horned, and sits at the far end of the table. I see her peeking over as she chats to a more-gothic-than-normal Órla. Next thing, Órla lets out a cackle of laughter the likes of which only she can excavate from a set of human lungs. Then Lorraine is laughing too. She pops over for a hug. 'I'm after asking Órla who's the ride,‡' she explains, all sheepish. 'You're allowed to fancy boy-me: he's a feek,§' I say, 'c'mon, let's have a boogie.'

How to dance as a boy. I know, instinctively, that I shouldn't move from my hips as usual. It's mad: it feels like that's where my rhythm is located, like, if I can't beat the music out with my hip bones, I can't really get it to reverberate through the rest of my body. I try to keep the music in my legs, try to keep my neck stiff. I scope out the other lords a-leaping. They're more angular in their movements than the ladies: more line, less circle. I copy them, developing a deadly little fien routine that feels enough like me to be fun without giving the girly game away (an occasion hip jab, I reckon, is allowed).

There's a freedom in being left alone by lads: of not being eyed-up, of not eyeing anyone up. But I'd be a liar if I said

---

* Oranmore village, where I'm from. The hippest, hoppest, happeningest place on Earth. Not.
† Girls
‡ Attractive person
§ Attractive male person

that I didn't miss it too. Mad how much a simple costume can change my experience of this oh-so-familiar club, this oh-so-familiar music, of familiar and unfamiliar faces.

I find my friends Susan and Marina on the dancefloor, done up as witchy cats or catty witches, depending. After the initial gasps and laughs, we get our groove on, and I become aware of a young lad skulking around the outside of our circle, waiting for a chance to pounce on pretty Suz. It's mischief I am, and as of yet clueless about rules between boys vying for girls on dancefloors. I wrap an arm around Suz and say: 'That's my girlfriend!' Susan laughs. Smooth and chivalrous as all get out,* our pal switches his amorous attentions to the lovely Marina, who is unimpressed entirely. So I wrap an arm around her next and say, 'That's my girlfriend, too!' The girls crack up. Then something unexpected happens.

The boy grabs my wrist, hard, and says, 'What the fuck are you playing at?' 'Ooow,' I say, 'let go, I'm only messing. I'm a girl!' He double takes, pulls my hat off and throws it on the ground, his eyes all fight. Suz tells him to piss off – can he not take a joke? I re-arrange my hat to conceal any stray and wispy blondie bits. Dancefloors, I am learning, are a different kind of minefield for men.

I'm two scoops† in, and I have a bladder-pressing di- lemma: to the gents or to the ladies? Ah feck it – in for a penny, in for a euro. I head for the lads' jacks. The smell of piss hits me on entry, but I've cleaned enough pub toilets in my time not to gag. I head for a cubicle, ignoring the

---

* 'as all get out' means very or extremely.
† Pints

backs at the urinals. I mean, I could *try* to pee standing up, but it's been a while. Me and Gráinne O'Toole (no relation) used to practise in her parents' ensuite when we were eight. We weren't that bad, if I remember rightly. But then, I also thought I was good at drawing when I was eight, and I definitely wasn't. Maybe Gráinne's mum spent hours cleaning wee off the floor after every visit, and thought me a very odd little girl altogether. Awenaise, if you don't use it, you lose it, and I didn't trust my eight-year-old gowl* aim to be in good nick, so I headed for a cubicle, where the graffiti hadn't half the sca† and soul-bearing of the Ladies'.

I feel awkward in this male space. I keep my eyes down as I wash my hands, and wonder if anyone will notice. Sure enough, one of the fellas waiting for a dryer says 'you're not a boy!' Corbed‡ – I freeze. 'I am, yeah,' I argue with an intentional lack of conviction, mustering the cheekiest of chappiness that I can muster. It's strange not to be able to rely on my femininity to create fun, friendly initial interactions with boys. 'Well you're the only lad I know has to draw on his bumfluff, like.' Feck it – the lights in the jacks are bright, and Sherlock has my number.

'Look man,' I say, 'Don't slag the goatee – I'm pretty self-conscious about my lack of beard. So yeah, I give myself a bit extra from time to time. Does that make me less of a man?' My new friend laughs, and his mate joins us. 'Hang on, I know her,' he says. He does look familiar (it's Galway

---

*   A rude word for female private parts
†   Story/Scandal
‡   Busted/Caught

– everyone looks familiar). 'Your name's Emer,' he says, 'you're cute!' I break character (he's cute too). 'Are you actually chatting me up beside the urinals?' 'Is she cute?' says the detective. 'Yeah man, sure look at the eyes.' The detective stares at my faux-bearded face under its Liverpool FC beanie cap. 'This is weirding me out,' he says, 'it's all kinds of wrong. I want to be looking, but I don't want to be looking. I'm getting out of the jacks before I go gay, like.'

So now I've been chatted up, while cross-dressing, in the men's toilet. Deadly. In 'Notes on "Camp"' which I'm after reading for Critical Theories in English, Susan Sontag says that what's most attractive in the masculine is an element of the feminine and what's most attractive in the feminine is an element of the masculine. The gents of Galway wouldn't be having any of that. But Susan Sontag probably didn't spend much time hanging out in the lads' jacks of The Warwick Hotel.

I'm heading to the bar for my third liquid treat of the evening when I see my good friend Eoin, a mature student from college, who I hang out with most days. I walk purposefully in his direction and shoulder-jostle him to see if I can psyche him out. Turns out he's older but no wiser than the rest. He turns slowly, pulls himself to the full extent of his five foot eleven inches, and squares up. I strike a comedic boxing pose, and he susses something's out of joint, looking to find clues in the little fella in front of him.

'Jesus, Emer,' he laughs, 'You look like a right gurrier.* I was ready for a fight.' 'Eoin, man,' I say in my girl voice,

---

* hooligan

'it's been the maddest night. I mean, I'm only wearing baggy clothes and a hat, I only have eyeliner on my face, but, like, everyone has fallen for it.' 'Yeah,' he says, 'it's cracked, because when you look properly, it's obviously you, and you're obviously a girl, but it's hard to see at first.'

I get back out on the dancefloor, where my friend Laura (currently vampiric) plays a joke on a friend of hers by pointing at me and telling her that I was asking if she was single. The friend dances on over for a better gander, throwing shapes.* Laura edges up and whispers in my ear that I have an admirer. 'Hey baby,' I say in a parody of Yankee masculinity, 'wanna jive?' I grab her hand and twirl her round (Boy-me is, like, smooth with the laydeez). Laura's pissing herself. Her friend looks for the dodge, and peers questioningly at us both. 'He's a girl!' Laura squeals (ever the excellent keeper of secrets), and her poor friend is so scarlet that she runs off the dancefloor. 'Laura,' I say, 'that wasn't nice.' 'It's Halloween,' she says, 'we're not supposed to be nice.'

The night is getting on, and Galway's scariest spooks and spirits sway to The Smiths and Belle and Sebastian on the Warwick dancefloor. Skeletons, zombies, witches, fairies and devils intersperse with conservatives costumed only as themselves. I shake my masculine thang. My movements remain abrupt, contained. My rhythm marches rather than skips. But then The Flaming Lips start playing, and I can't keep my hips under wraps. I let go and melt into feminine patterns, patterns I learned along the way to adulthood,

---

* To throw shapes is to make one's sexual interest known to a potential suitor in a non-verbal manner

and which I dance now without thinking. They feel natural, but really they're as formalised and feigned as my boyish grounded angularity. My wrists gyrate, and my arms and neck are fluid and delicate; my hips beat circles, first one way, then the other, my feet are free to point and my shoulders to roll. I am a girl dancing. I am a girl who looks like a boy dancing. And suddenly, I'm aware, I have a small audience.

I allow the music to wash from one body part to another, a dance I have rehearsed a thousand times, a performance long incorporated into my own idea of who I am. *This* is the way I dance. The small group of people who have stopped their grooving are watching my strange spectacle of androgyny unfold. And I wonder, vaguely, as I let my body do what it knows how to do, what I have had to work against it doing all night, if I look like a boy on the outside who's a girl on the inside? Or if I'm a mixture of masculinity and femininity? If I were dressed as my habitual Halloween sexpot, and if I adopted a masculine, soldierly dance, would this also attract an audience? Or is my masculinity only convincing because it's understated enough to draw minimum attention?

It is so much easier to act girly – that's the script I know – but tonight has shown me that girlness and boyness are performances, and I don't know how to begin sorting out what's me and what's an act – what I want to do, what makes me happiest, what makes the world a better place, and what I do because it's comfortable habit, easy routine. The Flaming Lips stop playing, and I'm still for a second. A guy from my small audience taps me on the shoulder.

'Excuse me,' he says, 'but that's the coolest thing I've ever seen.'

WHY DRAWN-ON BEARDS MAKE YOUR OLDEST GIRL-FRIENDS FANCY YOU

Cross-dressing nineteen-year-old me was just over five foot five inches, about eight and a half stone and disguised only with a hat, baggy clothing and a drawn-on beard. How and why did this not particularly cunning disguise confound and confuse her old compadres and new indie club compatriots alike? I've come to think about the answer through the psychological concept of schema.

We're receiving loads of new sensory information from the world around us all the time. We need ways to process this information – to decide what's important to focus on and what's not – otherwise we'd short circuit like poor Johnny Five. So we have beliefs and expectations based on prior experience and social conditioning and we make automatic judgements about most things, rather than considering them in detail.

In other words, we're all jumping to conclusions all the time. However, contrary to the way we usually think about jumping to conclusions, this can be a good thing. If we didn't have these reflexive cognitive reactions we'd have to consciously process every little thing as if we were experiencing it for the first time, and we'd spend from morning to midnight figuring out how to put on a clean pair of socks. Our brains are kind of lazy: they want the most useful answer with the least amount of work. And this has been good for us, in evolutionary terms. We're a species of pragmatists, not perfectionists.

Schema (plural: schemata) is a term used in psychology to describe a framework of beliefs or ideas about the world. It has been a mainstay of the way we understand human thought processes since Jean Piaget first theorised it in the late twenties. We use schemata to make judgements or to make sense of new information. A schema is built by a child's earliest encounters, then 'filled' with information that fits.

Here are some characteristics of schemata. First: they are self-fulfilling. This means that we're more likely to notice things that support our schema, and less likely to notice things that don't. So, Lorraine looks across a nightclub table at a human being in baggy clothes and a beanie hat, and these things match her schema of masculinity. She has jumped to a conclusion about the gender of the person across the table based on these shallow markers. She is now less likely to notice the petite size and dubious facial hair of the man opposite. Others in the club make the same flash judgement, and their cognitive processes attempt to uphold this judgement until the evidence for its incorrectness forces them to abandon it. This is why, as Eoin remarked, my femaleness, though obvious once revealed, was difficult to see at first.

Next, the content of a schema isn't always explicit, by which I mean that we're often unaware of the associations and shortcuts that our brain is making for us. Data from a technique called Implicit Association Testing* has shown that people who do not explicitly consider themselves to be racist or sexist often implicitly associate stereotypical concepts with people of colour or women. Many of us believe that we're colourblind when it comes to race, or egalitarian when it comes to gender, but at the most fundamental cognitive level, our schemata contain all sorts of prejudices.[26]

There's a riddle that is often used to illustrate the gender prejudice implicit in schemata. A father and son are in a terrible car crash. The father dies and the son is taken to hospital. But just as the boy is about to go under the knife, the surgeon exclaims, 'I can't operate! This is my son.' When researchers Mikhaela Wapman and Deborah Belle asked a group of 197 psychology students and 103 children (age seven to seventeen) to explain how this could be, they got all sorts of answers – including adoptive fathers, gay parents, unhinged medical professionals and even ghostly resurrections – before revealing that the surgeon is the boy's mother.

Only 15 per cent of the participants found their way to this conclusion. And self-professed feminists only did a little better, with 22 per cent getting the answer. For Wapman and Belle their participants' difficulty in imagining a surgeon

---

* Because our brains perform simple tasks quickly and complex tasks less quickly, IAT measures the response times of participants when associating certain people or groups with certain words or images. For example, if your race schema already associates people of colour with violence or women with irrationality, your response time to an association task based on these things will be comparatively speedy. If you'd like to participate in some IAT testing to see how it works and to contribute to science, you can go to www.implicit.harvard.edu. (Warning: it's pretty fun. You might lose an afternoon.)

mother is an effect of gender schemata, which do not reflect personal values or even major life experiences.[27]

Slightly tangentially (but importantly, I think): the implicit nature of the content of our schemata, combined with the fact that they are self-fulfilling, is part of why eye-witness accounts are sometimes considered to be unreliable court-room evidence and part of why people of colour often get heavier sentences for comparable crimes.[28]

Next characteristic: we're less likely to notice things that don't support our schema, and when we do notice them, we're less likely to believe them. When we encounter information that contradicts our schema we tend to cast it as an exception or add a caveat to our existing framework. So, for example, if I believe that women can't wee standing up, and I see a woman weeing standing up, I might a) think that she's not a cis-woman* peeing un-aided: she might have a penis; she might have bought herself one of those pee-funnels that are marketed to women at festivals or b) modify my schema slightly. In the case of b), if the woman is Irish and I've never met an Irish woman before I might alter my schema so that I now believe that women can't pee standing up, except for them unnatural Irish savages. It takes a significant amount of contrary information (like every woman I meet impressing me with her awesome upright urination skills) to make me abandon my schema entirely.

---

* A cis-gendered person is someone who experiences their gender in line with society's expectations for someone of their biological sex. The term arose from trans-sexual and transgender activism, both because it's less clunky than 'not-trans' and also because it helps us to stop thinking of cis-gender as normal and transgender as abnormal, and allows us to talk about both as valid ways of experiencing gender.

Schemata, as I've noted, are necessary and helpful. It would be impossible to function without making automatic judgements based on half-observations or shallow markers. But they also have an obvious downside, especially, as the data from Implicit Association Testing shows, when it comes to things like class, race or gender. When we encounter a person who has been coded as working class/middle class, black/white or masculine/feminine, we infer a vast range of other traits that society or experience has taught us to associate with these demographics. In other words, our schemata can be stereotypical, causing us to 'read' people in terms of prejudices instead of the information we have about them.

A psychologist whose work on gender schema I greatly admire is Sandra Bem (who sadly died aged only 70 just as I finished writing this book). She thinks of schemata as lenses through which we view the world, and uses the metaphor of 'gender lenses' for our tendency to read people in terms of gender stereotypes. Bem's work calls for people to look *at* gender lenses rather than *through* them: that is, to try to understand our subconscious prejudices before making judgements about women, men and society.[29]

In the seventies, Bem came up with the Bem Sex Role Inventory (BSRI), which drastically changed the way that psychologists thought about gender.[30] Prior to Bem, the accepted wisdom was that there was a gender scale, with masculinity at one end, and femininity at the other, and that people's psychological wellbeing and social adjustment was related to how well their gender psychology 'matched' their sex. So, according to this logic, you were either masculine or feminine. And feminine women were happiest. And masculine men were happiest.

The BSRI changed the game: it allowed for people to have masculine characteristics and feminine characteristics at the same time. Instead of one scale, there are two – a masculine scale and a feminine scale – and it's possible to score highly on one (making you masculine or feminine), to score highly on both (making you androgynous), or to score highly on neither (making you undifferentiated). And rather than finding that people whose gender identity matched their sex were best-adjusted (which was about 34 per cent of people), Bem found that the approximately 33 per cent of people who were a mixture of masculine and feminine characteristics – androgynous people – were best-adjusted. Later research that bounced off Bem's suggested that those androgynous people who combined the most positively-rated characteristics of masculinity and femininity were the best adjusted of all.*

People whose self-identification accords with their gender are 'sex-typed'. and people whose self-identification is opposite of their gender are 'cross-sexed typed' (about 8 per

---

* In her later work, Bem moves away from the concept of androgyny, and more towards the concept of gender schematicity. She says 'By the late 1970s and early 1980s I had begun to see that the concept of androgyny inevitably focuses so much more attention on the individual's being both masculine and feminine than on the culture's having created the concepts of masculinity and femininity in the first place that it can be legitimately said to reproduce precisely the gender polarization that it seeks to undercut. Accordingly, I moved on to concept of gender schematicity because it enabled me to argue even more forcefully that masculinity and femininity are merely the construction of a cultural schema – or lens – that polarises gender.' (Bem, Sandra. *The Lenses of Gender: Transforming the Debate on Sexual Inequality.* Yale UP: 1993. p. viii.)

cent of people).* Although this is something of a chicken and egg statement (because schemata are not innate, but built through early experience), sex-typed people are more likely to apply and uphold a stereotypical gender schema.

Androgynous, cross-sexed-typed and undifferentiated people are less likely to make judgements and hold beliefs based on a stereotypical gender schema. This has the upside of avoiding prejudice, and the downside of making the world a pretty confusing place some of the time. While this is again a chicken and egg statement, those of us with such psychologies are oftentimes left staring in blank distress at things that other people seem able to accept. We live with the eternal urge to shriek: 'Why? Why? Why are all the people with vaginas strapping three-inch spikes to their ankles in order to go dancing? Why do I have to remove my body hair? Why are we discussing Hillary Clinton's make-up routine instead of her foreign policy? NONE OF IT MAKES ANY SENSE!'

I've long thought that the idea of gender schema opens up radical possibilities in terms of challenging prejudices about women and men. If implicit stereotypical views about gender are backed up hourly, daily, by sensory information that people (mis)perceive according to their gender schema, then doesn't consistently playing with these outward signs, these shallow markers, have the power to make us confront our prejudices? At first, we might simply add a caveat to our existing schema. But continued disruption of our implicit

---

* The test also includes 'near feminine' and 'near masculine' scores, which accounted for about 26 per cent of people.

expectations must eventually lead to an awareness of our biases.

The conscious effort to disrupt gender schema that I'm advocating here doesn't have to mean that everyone joins me in staring blankly at society, barely containing the urge to shriek 'Why? Why? Why do all the dental hygienists have vaginas and all the plumbers have penises? Why are none of the people with penises allowed to wear skirts unless they're Scottish and there's a wedding? Why? Why? NONE OF IT MAKES ANY SENSE.' It doesn't mean that we wouldn't have any time-saving psychological devices with regard to understanding gender. It's just that our new schema would encourage us to feel outraged when confronted with stereotypes; it would tell us that we can assume very little about anyone based on their perceived masculinity, femininity or androgyny.

This is the conclusion that Bem comes to in her 1998 book *An Unconventional Family*, in which she talks about how to raise 'gender-liberated' children in an unequal world. She suggests teaching children to identify and critique gender stereotypes, and to judge individuals on their distinct and diverse individual behaviours rather than on markers like gender, race, class or sexual orientation. Imagine living in a world full of people who'd been raised like that.[31]

As I've said, people will modify and add caveats to a schema for a long time before contrary information forces them to abandon it. And so, changing the expectations and beliefs of adults is, in ways, a harder project than teaching children to develop egalitarian schema in the first place. But what feminist doesn't like a challenge?

IT'S ALL DRAG

In 1990, Naomi Wolf said that to battle the kind of oppression that manifests not in official legislation but in the very fabric of the way we live, women need more than the placards and slogans of first-wave feminists: we need new ways to see.[32] How can we remove the blinkers, adjust the lenses? Should we go completely wild, and anarchically reject every norm of our society for which we can't see an egalitarian logic?

Bakhtin's notion of the Carnivalesque hints that this won't work. A total lack of norms will only make people long for the stability of conformity, regardless of the inequality that is the price of that stability. Equality can't just be chaos. No one wants a year of Mardi Gras.[33]

The Carnivalesque is a time without any ideologies or politics, and so it doesn't really have the potential to change society. It's more like a safety valve: it lets everyone blow off the steam that builds up because their lives are structured by unfair, illogical rules. If your aim is to try to think about ways to change society, just encouraging everyone to go loolah once in a while isn't going to work. It's only going to make them want to go back to something safe and structured and functional, even though it is the structured, functional society that makes them want to go loolah now and again.

First in 1984 and again in 2000, Bell Hooks called for a return to a revolutionary – rather than a reformist – feminism.[34] She meant that simply having the right to act like men in a system built on hierarchy and oppression isn't enough. We need to make radical changes to the way in which our society is structured. I believe that one of the roads towards doing this is to unsettle implicit gender bias using our bodies. We must single out the norms that seem the most harmful, play with them, poke fun at them, and ultimately change them.

Choose Halloween. Pick a costume. Experiment with gender: make it a game. This isn't as frivolous as it sounds: the experience of this performance – of this costume – highlights the ways in which we are always performing, we are always in costume.

Once I was a girl dancing. Once, I was a girl dressed as a boy dancing as a girl. I was an act acknowledging that I was an act, in so many competing and conflicting layers that neither I, nor anybody else, knew where the act began or ended. It was the coolest thing.

This is the radical potential of performing gender differently. You're bringing the 'act' of it all, the creativity of it all, the arbitrariness of it all, to the surface. You're bouncing balls off people's schema. You're graffiti-ing their gender lenses. And when you've got a taste for this, rewriting the script of everyday life begins to seem less daunting. You feel increasingly ready to take your performance into the realm of the 'real'. You've moved beyond noticing that things don't have to be as they are, to acting as though they are not, to creating a world in which others must also acknowledge new gender possibilities, a world in which we are not, primarily, women and men, but people.

It's only costume. It's only play. It's only an act. *We* are only costume, *we* are only play, *we* are only an act. Once we've been given the choreography of gender, there is no naked. It's all drag.

CHAPTER FOUR:

REPRESENTING REALITY BITES

*'The task of the postmodern feminist is to lay bare
and contest the discursive construction of all seemingly
stable categories.'*
Margrit Shildrick and Janet Price[35]

CHASING DREAMS IN THE BIG CITY

I repeated the cross-dressing experiment a few more times
in Galway, outside of the safe parameters of Halloween. I
learned more about gender, performance and perception,
and had a thoroughly entertaining time doing so. But it
wasn't all plain sailing round Galway Bay. My hometown
is an odd mixture of artiness and conservatism, consist-
ing of approximately 70,000 people who see too much of
each other. Given that this was also around the time in my
life when I started to explore my sexuality, I built up an
interesting reputation, based in germ on fact and in majority
on Galway's rumour mill, which is capable of producing
Pulitzer Prize-standard fiction in forty-eight hours or less.
Take this dude:

'Hey, your name's Emer.'

'Hey, yeah, have we met?'

'Yes. Well no. But I see you at The Warwick sometimes.'

'Yeah, Strange Brew's my buzz.'

'One time, weren't you dressed as a boy?'

'I've done that a few times. It's fun.'

'And weren't you there with your girlfriend?'

'Em, if you mean Máire, I don't think she was with me actually, no . . .'

'She definitely was.'

'I really don't . . .'

'And then your boyfriend showed up.'

'Hang on – that was a different night. I wasn't dressed as a boy. And I wasn't really going out with either Máire or Cyril . . .'

'And then they got in a fist-fight.'

'Okay, that didn't happen . . .'

'And your girlfriend won . . .'

'Okay . . .'

'And then your boyfriend ran off down the road shouting "fucking lesbians" except no one knew what he was talking about because you looked like a man.'

'I see.'

'That was cool.'

'Uh-huh.'

So, by the time I was 22, it was necessary to move to Dublin – a sprawling metropolis of 1 million people – where the streets would be paved with tolerance, and I could exist in relative anonymity as I subtly adjusted my gender lenses. Shortly after I quit the kooky yet beloved town of my birth I shaved off all my hair for the first time.

My official reason for this exercise in androgyny was that Dublin was expensive, and I couldn't afford the upkeep on my bleach-blonde pixie cut. As those of us who've been peroxide are aware: there is no way out that doesn't involve hours under those beehive things in hairdressers, adding ludicrously pricey highlights and lowlights, breathing in toxic fumes, feeling your scalp disintegrate and gradually going insane.

So, at a stupid o'clock in the morning party, my friend Tadhgh, at my casual behest, sheared me like a particularly co-operative sheep. Some partygoers cheered, while some tried their darndest to dissuade me with lies such as 'but you have lovely hair!' Tadhgh buzzed and I laughed and, unbeknownst to me, my friends Cillian and Darragh gathered up all the blonde clippings, put them in an envelope, and posted it to me at the awful hotel where I was working that summer. I was bald. I remember looking in the mirror and thinking how strange it was that I still looked like me. *More* like me, somehow – as though my face had nowhere to hide.

Shaving my head was something I'd been considering for about a year, as a kind of gender challenge to myself. It was all well and good playing dress-up, but could I rock a drastically different costume in real life? The folks at the awful hotel didn't know what to make of it, and, as my bar staff uniform consisted of black slacks, a stripy shirt and a tie, I habitually got mistaken for a boy by the customers (I'll take that apology in tips, thanks missus). A few months later, I quit my hotel job and started a Master's degree in Theatre and Performance at Trinity College Dublin, my spikey hairdo held ever-so stylishly in place with wetlook Brylcreem.

While my adventures in cross-dressing taught me in a blatant way that people make snap decisions about gender based on shallow markers, my Sinéad O'Connor tribute scalp taught me similar lessons in a much more nuanced fashion. This time, I wasn't in disguise: I just had a culturally unusual haircut. And because I wasn't in disguise, people's reactions were more 'real' ('reality', someone clever once said, is the only word which always belongs in quotation marks). I was exactly the same person, but I was now being judged – in very profound and integral ways – on the length of the dead proteins protruding from my scalp.

For one thing, people read me as more aggressive. And this was a sea change because, due to my innocent fawn eyes, I have long been renowned for looking about a million times sweeter than I actually am. I've never been a shrinking violet, but before I shaved my luscious locks I never had anyone react to me with actual fear.

Isn't it amazing what a short back and sides can do? At a family friend's wedding, where I was rocking my head spikes with a pair of killer stilettos and a pretty frock, a guy turned to my big brother as I tore up the dancefloor and said 'See that girl over there? She's very attractive, but I think she'd cut my balls off.' To which poor Ronan could only really reply, in a tone I can only really imagine: 'that's my sister.'

Another thing that happened was that people assumed I was psychologically unstable. Because I'd chosen to adopt a normatively masculine hairstyle, a significant number of people thought I must be depressed or otherwise mentally ill. Bem's sex role index might have debunked the correlation of gender conformity and mental wellbeing in scientific circles, but it was alive and kicking in the real world. I tried to counter this assumption by smiling and laughing a lot, which may have helped – or may just have proffered the proof people needed.

Also interesting was that the world started to make assumptions about my sexuality. Suddenly, I was socially gay. I remember hanging out in Dublin's Front Lounge – which is a gay-friendly straight bar or a straight-friendly gay bar, depending on who you ask – and trying to courteously ignore what I took to be the advances of a man with bad energy beside me. But he got me on the guilt card: he said, 'it doesn't cost anything to be nice, you know.'

Then I felt bad for being snooty, so I apologised and explained that I'd had some unpleasant experiences chatting with strangers at bars, so I could be a bit cautious, and asked whether he was having a good night and all that. The shifty-eyed sleaze said, 'it's okay. I know what kind of a place this is. I know what kind of a girl you are. I just wanted to tell you that you look like a very sensuous woman.' Shudder.

And as I made my way back to my friends, feeling as though I'd been covered in ectoplasm, I thought how strange it was that my shaved head was enough to pigeonhole me in this neither straight nor gay space. And I was vaguely angry that, once Slimer had decided I was gay based on the incontrovertible evidence of my hairstyle, he felt he had the right to my friendly attention. He wasn't trying to score me, after all, just to make puke-inducing comments about my presumed sensuality. Then I had a pint and a laugh and got over it.

A final notable change in the way the world reacted to my new tressless incarnation was that I received a lot less sexual attention. Heads did not turn and horns did not honk. And I missed it. I wanted it. I remember the knock to my confidence, and how difficult it was to feel good about myself. Once, an attractive, interesting young man asked if he could share my table when the Trinity sandwich bar was busy. We ended up talking for two hours, after which he asked me to e-mail him the play I'd just finished writing.

It didn't occur to me that he might have been interested in anything other than reading my script (which was all in rhyming verse, and was about a girl hiding in a library because a French perfume company patented the smell of strawberries. It remains unstaged). I was bowled over when he later asked me out for a drink. Isn't it sad that I believed that my looks were the only reason a man might be interested in me: that I took head turns and horn honks as valid expressions of interest, yet couldn't compute attention based on my (dubious) creativity, (in embryo) intellect, or (de facto) warmth and humour? I'll answer that: yes it is.

Shaving my head for the first time was not a feminist act, but it kissed my feminist consciousness awake for good. Because I came to see that if people were assuming that I was aggressive because of a shaved head, they had equally been assuming that I was passive because of long hair. If they were assuming that I was unhappy and unstable because of this small act of gender non-conformity, they were equally assuming that my habitual conformist femininity was a symbol of social adjustment and psychological wellbeing. If my short hair made people pigeonhole me as homosexual, my long hair, then, made people pigeonhole me as heterosexual. Long hair, short hair, conformist, non-conformist, feminine, masculine: I was being gender stereotyped all the time. Suddenly, I had a new way to see.

A shaved head is a symbol. Long hair is a symbol. And symbols are important – they dictate the ways that others read us, what they expect from us, and how they feel entitled to treat us. In important ways, they shape our realities. And so it's important to stop and think about this powerful kind of cultural communication.

What's represented by striving to be thin, wearing high heels, wearing make-up, spritzing perfume, adorning ourselves with accessories? I'm not going to attempt a symbolic breakdown of all of these costumes of womanhood: I presume my reader is more than capable of that herself. But I'm reminded of a joke that a man once told me at a music festival: Why do women wear perfume and make-up? Because they are smelly and ugly. And while this is obviously flippant (and funny), is there an extent to which our performances of these gendered behaviours communicates that we believe ourselves to be substandard? Is there an extent to which they symbolise that to be a woman is to be concerned with shallow things, decorative things, the stuff of costume and disguise, not the stuff of substance and 'reality'?

If so, we have a dilemma because, what's a girl to do? Reject the trappings of femininity entirely? Should we shave our heads, invest in Monday-thru-Sunday dungarees, bin our MAC eyeshadow, and then – holding hands and chanting – burn everything frilly we own in a bonfire of ascetic feminist commitment, our bare scalps glinting in the revolutionary flames? While that sounds fun (I'll bring the Pimm's), I have a feeling it'd be counter-productive.

For one thing, costuming ourselves to accord with society's stereotypical idea of what buzz-kill feminists look like isn't going to crack anyone's gender lenses. And for another, the problem – I believe – isn't the symbols; rather, it's what they represent. Long hair shouldn't signify passivity any more than short hair should signify aggression. Make-up shouldn't signify frivolity any more than a closely shaved chin or a well-trimmed beard. The problem is not skirts, stilettos or other symbols of femininity; rather, it's what the symbols of femininity mean in our sexist culture.

The answer, then, might be to manipulate the symbols: to play with them and mix them up. Manipulating gendered symbols in everyday life is more than a performance: it's more than fiction. It is a strategy that blurs the line between representation and reality, by shaking fixed and stable ideas of what women and men are and how they should behave.

STRANGER THAN FICTION

Symbols are a means of communication. A circle on top of a triangle on a bathroom door is a symbol for a woman, and it communicates that only women should wee behind that door (not directly behind the door, silly). But why is a circle on top of a triangle a symbol for a woman? Because we know it stands for a person in a dress, and we know that people in dresses are usually female. In order to work, symbols require a substantial degree of knowledge of the society in which we live.

Sometimes symbols cease to have the same relationship with reality that they used to, yet they continue to work because people understand them. Not all women wear dresses. Yet the symbol is effective, because everyone knows what it means. There's a sense in which the symbol here (circle + triangle) has been cut loose of what it signifies (woman).

We have the 'reality' – that there is nothing inevitable about the connection between women and skirts – and then we have the symbol – through which women are represented by skirts. The symbol is not intrinsically related to what it represents. Rather, it is related to what we all know that it means.

What about when you are *wearing* the symbol – perhaps a skirt, perhaps a shaved head, perhaps make-up? In that case, the symbol is communicating something to the world about your identity, about who you are. But, of course, your audience – the world at large – needs social knowledge in order to interpret it and act accordingly.

The thing is, none of these symbols are actually tied to the 'reality' of who someone is, nor to the biological fact of being female or male. They are tied instead to a shared system of knowledge and beliefs. And we can manipulate symbols to make the world ascribe certain identities to us. We can costume ourselves, and we can perform. So where is the 'real' in all of this? Where is the authentic, the natural, the feminine, the 'me'? What is truth and what is fiction? What are the boundaries of our gender performances?

One of the most interesting things about our era is the degree to which the line between representation and 'reality' has been blurred. On TV, we're bombarded with an array of 'reality' shows, which we know are heavily scripted. When two characters from *The Only Way is Essex* meet to discuss their latest romantic infidelities, we know that the encounter has been staged and lit and is being filmed, and so there is no way that these people – even if they are friends in 'real' life – can be acting naturally.

Yet, there are scripts for how we should behave in our everyday lives too. Some conversations are appropriate with Great-Aunt Jacinta; some are not. We costume ourselves differently for different scenes. On the streets, in shops, in restaurants or in offices, our behaviours are recorded by CCTV. At parties, we're recorded by our friends' smart-phones. Online, our surfing habits are recorded by search engines. Recent revelations of government surveillance of civilians mean that we're conscious someone could always be watching. So tell me: can we be acting naturally?

The performance theorist Neil Gabler talks about phe-nomena he calls 'lifeys', where real life events – the Oscar Pistorius murder trial is a good contemporary example – get turned into a form of entertainment by media outlets. Lifeys are the new hit shows, the new blockbusters. We are all awaiting the next instalment. Real people become characters: quoted, photographed and filmed in ways that will hook audiences. Gabler says that while once there was a line between art and life, and we used to escape from reality into representation, now we escape from life into more life, from reality into more reality.[36]

These understandings – that symbols are not attached to reality but rather to agreements we share about what they mean; that the line between fact and fiction is blurry at best – are part of what is called in academia 'the postmodern condition'.[37]

Postmodernism is an ongoing philosophical movement concerned with deconstructing binaries. It questions apparently stable oppositional categories (such as black/white; good/evil; male/female; master/slave; fact/fiction) that structure our thought and our society and, in doing so, allows new ways of thinking and living to emerge. Deconstructing binary gender roles has been a major postmodern concern, as gender is one of the most fervently defended and policed binaries in our culture.

Binary categories used to be explained through religion. God made kings rich and peasants poor; God made women to serve men; God made the different races of humanity and put them on different continents; God is good; the Devil is bad. However, from the late seventeenth century (an intellectual time known as The Enlightenment), Western culture began to put its faith in reason over religion and superstition. We were learning more about the world around us than ever before, and the things we were learning could be proved scientifically. Aristocracy was on the decline and democracy was on the up. People believed that humanity was progressing towards a more rational, just and equal future.

Binaries continued to structure Western thought and culture, but now the binaries were legitimated through reason and science. For example, it was widely believed that men and women or black people and white people had extremely different psychologies and that this could be scientifically proven by looking at the size and shape of their brains.

Postmodernism arose when these kinds of certainties finally crumbled in the first half of the twentieth century. The early twentieth century, with its two horrific wars, shattered belief in Western progress. The world was shown that new technologies could be used to kill hundreds of thousands of young men in the trenches. The efficiency of industrialisation could be used to transport six million Jews and two million others, including people of colour and gay people, to factories that produced only death. 'Sciences' like Eugenics (the science of improving human stock) and Phrenology (the science of measuring the brain to determine intellectual capabilities) could be used to justify the greatest barbarism of all: genocide.

The late nineteenth and early twentieth century also brought decolonisation. African, Indian, Asian and indigenous thinkers pointed their fingers at the greed that was the real reason for Europe's supposedly noble task of civilising the world, and asserted that there was nothing inferior about their cultures. Roughly at the same time, the political movements of people of colour, women and the working classes were shouting that the 'progress' of Western society was not based on reason at all, but on the unpaid or underpaid work of oppressed people.

And so the binaries that had been justified by religion before the Enlightenment and science after it were finally called into question. The age of reason was over.

Postmodernism blossomed from this uncertainty. As a philosophy, it accepts that there may be no objective truth and that advancing human scientific knowledge may not mean human progress. For postmodernists, there is no absolute right, there is no absolute wrong, there is no fact, there is no fiction: there's nothing but what we construct and agree to. Every apparently stable category, every 'common sense' and incontrovertible truth, is fair game for questioning and imagining anew.

Some people, of course, do still understand our socially constructed gender roles in terms of religion or pseudo-science. For example, many Christians believe that God made Eve as a helper for Adam, and so women should serve and obey men. Or, as Cordelia Fine points out, people will try to argue that little girls prefer pink and little boys prefer blue due to the different functioning of their brains. This is in spite of the fact that the association of girls with pink and boys with blue is only about sixty years old and, in Victorian times, little boys were dressed in pink (considered a strong, active colour) and little girls in blue (considered dainty and delicate).[38]

Humans like black and white: we like categories, answers, simple truths. We like to make order from chaos. So it's no wonder that some use religion or pseudoscience to explain the socially constructed identities that feel normal – even inevitable – to us. Some people prefer not to question at all; some get angry and derisive when you ask them why gender norms should be as they are.

But for many of us today, neither religion nor reason upholds the division between men and women in our society, and we're not afraid to question the rationale behind gender roles. When we do question, we often find that the rationale is sexism, not godliness or logic. We see that gender norms are limiting for everyone, and disadvantageous for women. The strangest thing for me, then, is that even when we see this and know this, we continue to play our parts, continue, through our bodies and our behaviours, to behave in conventionally feminine or masculine ways and prop up the gender binary.

Perhaps we do this because it's hard to imagine alternatives. Or perhaps we can't deal with uncertainty, with the realisation that there is no correct way to be a woman or a man, that, when it comes to how best to perform your gender under patriarchy, only you have the right answer for you. Life can be bewildering without the binaries and certainties that governed it before, but it also offers greater freedom to create our own worldviews, identities and 'realities'. When you look at it that way, postmodernism is kind of a party.

So go to the party and genderbend gently. Wear men's deodorant until it has stopped smelling masculine and just smells like you. Lower your voice on the phone – are people reacting to you differently? How? Bring it up a few pitches. Now? Wear men's underwear. Get a man to wear yours. Sing the bass line. Order the stout. Follow it with a sex on the beach. Grow one set of nails long and paint them, and keep the others trimmed and bare (great for guitarists). Hold doors open for men; help friends into their coats after dinner. Know how to change a bike tyre *and* how to bake cupcakes; don't give a crap how to put up shelves *or* how to knit a shrug. Pay for your date when they nip to the bathroom at the end of the meal. Surprise the world. Surprise yourself.

Or go to the party and genderbend hardcore. Dress in men's clothes, walk with a male gait, get a boy's hair cut, wear bright pink lipstick and false eyelashes: confuse things. Complement a sexy dress with hairy legs and hiking boots. Dress in full female drag – foam breasts, wig, outrageous platforms, queen-ish make-up – and go to a drag night: you're a girl, pretending to be a boy, pretending to be a girl. Isn't it fun? Give your male friends girly makeovers. Find a queer club night. Hit the town. Your body is political – you're using it to laugh at social norms, to expose their arbitrariness, and your performance is putting the theatricality of gender centre stage. No one can ignore it now.

Manipulating symbols like this is playful, but it's play with a purpose: it's playing with the gender binary. Remember that gendered symbols are not attached to a material reality, but to agreements we share about what they mean. So it is up to us to think about how we costume and code ourselves, and how we perform. It's up to us to think about which feminine symbols we want to reclaim, reinvent or celebrate, and which we want to throw on the scrap heap of sexism. Considering the relationship between reality and representation like this can be immensely empowering – it means, in the absence of objective truth about what it means to be a man or a woman, we can create the identities we want to have and the world we want to see. It means there are no limits to our gender performances.

CHAPTER FIVE:

OUT OF COSTUME

'Our bodies are ourselves: yet we are also more than our bodies.'

Lynda Birke[39]

SO TAKE OFF ALL YOUR CLOTHES

I am naked. I am one of two-and-a-half-thousand naked people curled into the foetal position on the damp stone of Dublin's South Wall pier. It's somewhere between five and six in the morning, and the bloodshot dawn has faded into a traditionally cold, wet, Irish summer's day. Waves throw themselves against the dock like moshing metal heads. The sea stretches out in front, grey water and cloud consubstantiating in the middle distance.

A Mexican wave of laughter ripples up and down the carpet of bodies, sometimes exploding around me, sometimes echoing far away. An insect crawls across my thigh. I close my eyes. It's a moment of my life from which I wouldn't be surprised to wake up.

In May 2008, the recruitment posters appeared around the city, shaking up the capital with images of photographer

Spencer Tunick's mass urban nudes. Tunick was travelling the globe and organizing groups of volunteers into incredible still shots against their urban environments. His work asked questions about the relationship between nature and culture, about industrialisation and modernity, about social norms and what it looks like when they are cast away. Needless to say, I was a big fan. I knew I wanted to take part, but getting naked with thousands of other people sounded scary.

'Are you brave enough, Dublin?' the bold print on the posters asked. I was brave enough with back-up, I decided, so I called my inhibitionless friend Mia. Her answer was 'Yes, yes, yes!' And so it was settled: on Saturday 23 June, in the name of art, we'd be stripping to the pelt at some mystery location in dear old dirty Dublin's docklands.

The date arrived, as dates will tend to do. Mia and her little sister Anna hopped on an evening bus from Galway to Dublin, while I spent the hours before their arrival convincing Sinéad, a girl I was seeing, that nocturnal nude modelling was the way forward. At about 11 p.m., Sinéad and I met Mia and Anna off their bus and brought them back to my tiny Northside flat for a nutritious pre-shoot meal of cheese on toast and vodka smoothies. 'I've never seen a naked man before,' said Anna, just eighteen, and we all agreed that a mass, urban, nude photoshoot would be a strange and wonderful way to change that.

At 3 a.m. we made our way to Custom House Quay to await transport to our mystery location, and half an hour later we were on a bus full of soon-to-be nudists. There was lots of singing (including a particularly memorable rendition of The Sultans of Ping's 'Where's Me Jumper?'), and occasional flashing of the bus behind. 'Gosh, it's hot in here,' someone innocently remarked, to a predictable chorus of 'SO TAKE OFF ALL YOUR CLOTHES!'

We arrived on site and spilled out into salty air and bracing winds. Dawn light melted over the stormy sea in happy berry-hued defiance. A Viking-bearded man with a megaphone rounded us up and herded us towards the water. The girls and I found a spot to sit, and swapped drinks, smokes and names with the folks around us. Helpers distributed fliers detailing the poses we'd be asked to adopt, and we practised them – parodying, laughing.

The command came, and the whole gaggle – all of us obediently clothed in public every other day of our lives – stripped. Suddenly I was in an army of pasty naked Paddies being whipped by the wind, marching away from the convention of clothing and to the very end of the South Wall pier. In front – backs and bottoms; behind – chests and bellies, faces, hair and skin. Mia and Anna whooped and skipped. I smiled a series of disbelieving grins at people I'd made small talk with, clothed, just moments before. They grinned back: we were all in something together.

I looked at the thousands of bodies marching and jiggling and skipping and stamping. A man in front of me came equipped with what looked for all the world like Beyoncé's bum. A slim and glamorously made-up woman to my right sported a tummy that hung down to her mid-thighs. A bloke close by was cheating, as his complete coat of dark, thick body hair meant that he couldn't be nearly as cold as the rest of us. Pendulous breasts swung. Concave chests scooped the wind like ice cream. Tiny torsos rested atop elephantine legs, while barrel bodies balanced precariously on stiletto-slim calves. There was no normal.

And it seemed stupid, all of a sudden, to divide the world into men and women, as if the most important difference between any two of these bodies was the bit between the legs. Because, genitalia aside, whose body did mine more closely resemble? That of the woman with full hips and breasts galloping up the pier in front of me? Or that of the pigeon-chested, elfin young man padding along behind?

Later in my life, reading feminist theory, I'd learn that I wasn't the first to remark upon the strangeness of acting as though biological sex is the single greatest difference between human bodies, when a mere sidewise glance at humanity should tell us that men and women come in such variety. Outside of the extremes of masculine and feminine characteristics there is such overlap between men and women, and there are so many factors other than biological sex that make human bodies similar or different to each other.

Moira Gatens talks about how bodies' 'histories' in terms of diet, environment and typical activities create their capacities, desires and material forms.[40] She says that the body of a wife and mother may have very little in common with the body of a female Olympic athlete, and that the body of a female Olympic athlete may have much in common with the body of a male Olympic athlete. This commonality isn't just about the kinds of activities that the people in these bodies are interested in and likely to carry out, but also in the way their bodies look and move, and the very things that they are capable of. Men's lives make men's bodies more manly; women's lives make women's bodies more womanly.

In the Dublin Docklands thousands of strippers stood in place to be photographed as they filled the pier. Tunick and his camera rocked on a boat in the choppy sea, and he called out instructions with a megaphone, asking us to form four staggered lines. We spread out, losing the defence of body heat, and discovered en masse the insulation limitations of human skin.

The bad weather made things difficult for the artist, and we waited for what seemed like an eternity, amazed at and inspired by each others' powers of endurance. I ran on the spot. Mia and Anna danced. Sinéad shook out her arms and legs. An empty passenger ferry glided past. 'Help,' Mia shouted to the liner, 'we've been here for days!'

Our first pose was standing facing out towards the sea, and I now keep a copy of the resultant shot on my living-room wall, where the pinks and whites and occasional browns of Irish skin melt into each other, and people look like pebbles lining the sea: each different, and yet so similar that, if you squint, they all look the same.

For the second pose, everyone sat, leaning back on their palms, faces upturned, like a cult of deluded sun-worshippers. For the third, we curled in to the foetal position, where I shut my eyes and listened as the jokes and laughter rumbled. There was distant chuckling. 'They must've Dylan Moran down there,' someone quipped, igniting cackles around me. My skin was numb, and the moment tingled.

Finally, after what must have been an hour in the nip,

we gave in, and, in one mind, began the long retreat back to our clothes. Everyone had been challenged by the biting wind, but there was a mood of celebration. I heard people marvelling and learning about humanity, society, convention and bodies, as though things were dawning on them that simply hadn't before. 'It's weird,' someone said, 'I'm not wearing any clothes, but I don't feel naked.'

LET'S TALK ABOUT BIOLOGICAL SEX, BABY

I've talked about gender as a kind of costume and learned – though deeply entrenched – way of performing. And already in this chapter I've talked about my feeling that when you look at the sheer variety of human bodies, it seems weird to divide them up, primarily, into male and female, as though the most significant difference between human beings is the kind of reproductive organs they possess. So I guess that a decently high proportion of readers are, by this stage, thinking to themselves: there might be elements of gendered behaviour that are performed, sure, and there might be similarities and differences between human bodies other than biological sex, sure, but the fact remains that some people are biologically, materially speaking men, and some people are biologically, materially women. Am I trying to say this isn't so?

Of course not. Some people are biologically male and some people are biologically female – that's a fact of biological sex. What I'm saying is that the social norms based on this fact are often unequal and often bear little logical relation to the physical and intellectual capacities of human bodies and human minds – that's a problem of gender. Also, it's important not to uncritically accept the idea that all human bodies can be neatly slotted into male and female categories. Like gender, biological sex is a spectrum, and there are intersex people too.

Intersex is the term used when a body doesn't fit into normative definitions of either male or female. There are lots of different reasons that people might be considered intersex – from having atypical genitalia to having mosaic chromosomes (where some of the chromosomes are XX and some XY). Also, there's much medical disagreement over what counts as intersex in the first place. Because of all this, it's difficult to say how common intersex people are, but the Intersex Society of North America (ISNA) approximates that 1 in 100 babies are born with anatomies that differ from typical male and female, and their research looks pretty solid to me.[41]

When you read that stat, did you think (as I did the first time I read it): 1 in 100? But that's 1 per cent – being intersex is really quite common. Where are all the intersex people? Why don't I know any? Why isn't there an intersex gender option when I'm asked to fill out a personal form? Why isn't there an intersex bathroom stall? The reason is that – while institutions such as the ISNA are working hard against this trend – intersex people are erased from our culture.

Where, for example, a child is born with ambiguous genitalia (approximately 1 or 2 in 1000 babies), parents, guided by medical teams, are often put under pressure to make a decision about 'corrective' genital surgery very shortly after birth – sometimes within twenty-four hours. Parents whose children are less visibly intersex (chromosomally intersex, for example) are under pressure to specify a sex on the birth certificate. Most children born intersex are not brought up as intersex, but as either boys or girls, though many change this identification in later life.

This pressure on parents to operate promptly on an intersex child with ambiguous genitalia, to specify a sex for an intersex baby, or to bring an intersex child up as either a boy or a girl is based on the belief that a child who isn't brought up in accordance with society's gender norms will be psychologically harmed. What toys should they play with? Should they hang out with boys or girls? What toilet should they use? What changing room? What clothes should they wear? Which sports team should they join? Should they try out for Eliza Doolittle or Henry Higgins in the school musical? How would they negotiate a first romantic or sexual relationship? And so I can understand, in a way, why the medical establishment advocates making a decision as to the sex of the child early on humanistic grounds. But I don't buy the logic.

For one thing, in adulthood, many intersex people find the fact that decisions about their gender were made when they were too young to consent the most traumatic thing of all. For another, the real problem is that society excludes intersex people, and, therefore, it is *society* that we should 'correct,' not the bodies of intersex children. Surely raising awareness of the existence of intersex people and fostering social acceptance would be a better way of preventing psychological harm than operating on babies' genitals?

But our society doesn't want to admit the existence of intersex people. Parents are not really told that it's an option to answer 'no' to the question: 'is Robin a little girl or a little boy?' A film scholar friend of mine, Dr Charlotte Gleghorn, recently wrote an article about the Brazilian film, *XXY*, about an intersex teenager who, confronted with her first love affair, has to make decisions about her bodily difference. In all the reviews for the film, the critics refer to the character as a hermaphrodite, even though she isn't (a hermaphrodite has both male and female reproductive organs). Charlotte says that this is because for most people, the idea of an intersex body is something mythical and unreal.[42]

Another friend of mine, Dr Felicity Gee (to whom I'm greatly indebted for this information on intersex), lectures on representations of intersex in film, and she once told me that, prior to her classes, the majority of her students hadn't been aware that intersex people existed. This is hardly surprising: in most countries intersex is not recognised as a gender option on personal records, and some intersex people don't have the right to marriage or civil partnerships, adoption or surrogacy, and are not permitted to complete the census. (This is slowly changing, and third gender or indeterminate gender legal status is now recognised to varying extents in countries including Australia, New Zealand, Germany, Bangladesh, India, Nepal and Pakistan.)

Why has physical sexual ambiguity been so rigorously erased from our culture? Why do we think of sex as a binary, while the existence of intersex people and the obvious variety of masculine and feminine characteristics across male and female bodies tell us that it's a spectrum? The answer to this, I believe, is that our society is unequal, and bodily difference is used to justify that inequality. Acknowledging intersex, coming to see biological sex as a spectrum rather than a binary, and becoming aware that gender is not defined by biology undermines that justification: it threatens people who believe that social inequalities between men and women are natural and inevitable.

LET'S TALK ABOUT GENDER, BABY

Biological sex is not as simple as X and Y, but most people do have an identifiable biological sex. What should a person's biological sex tell us about their gender identity? That is, what should it tell us about what kind of people they are, about how they are likely to act, and about the social roles they are cut out to play?

It's probably easiest to approach the question of gender identity by starting, first and foremost, with identity itself. What is identity? Is it a solid, interior thing – some stable core of 'me-ness' or 'you-ness'? Or is it something that is made up of the things you say and the things you do – is identity the way you perform?

I used to think the former – that I had an immutable self, which my actions could either authentically represent or betray. And, in fact, one of the earliest writers to attempt what I am attempting in *Girls Will Be Girls* takes the idea of an essential self as given. Erving Goffman wrote a famous (and horrendously sexist) book called *The Presentation of the Self in Everyday Life*. It uses the idea of social performance, of everyday theatre, to explain people's behaviours and habits.[43]

Goffman always assumes that there is an internal identity, and reads the actions of the people he studies (mostly Shetland Islanders, oddly) as kinds of performed negotiations between this essential identity and social expectations. And this makes sense because we do experience a lot of things privately, and we do behave in public or professional situations in ways that we wouldn't behave in private or casual ones (I'm picking my nose right now). But, as with so many things, life has managed to change my mind on the nature of identity.

When my Granny O'Toole was dying she needed 24-hour care, and I helped out with looking after her about once a week or once a fortnight towards the end (an experience which, by the way, has led me to believe that full-time carers are made entirely out of Black Forest gateaux and fairy dust). While Granny was the most selfless person you could imagine before she became physically incapacitated, when she was nearing death she was anxious and afraid – of course she was, it must be petrifying to be completely *compos mentis* and not to be able to do anything for yourself – and so she became very demanding and, honestly, difficult to be around.

Granny had an electric bell and each night I stayed with her, she'd ring it maybe eight, nine, ten times. She rang it because she was afraid that no one would come if she rang it; she didn't actually need anything. But then she'd make something up: I need a drink of water, or I need my pillow adjusted. Because she couldn't just say 'I need to know that you'll come if I call.' Sad, right? And, in retrospect, I'm so glad that I could've been there when she needed someone.

At the time, though, on the sixth call of the night, at four in the morning, knowing that there was nothing wrong with Granny at all, the sound of that bloody electric bell filled me with incandescent anger. My internal monologue shrieked, 'she doesn't NEED anything! It's four in the morning! It's a good job she's dying, 'cause otherwise I'd fecking kill her.' But I'd get up, and speak softly, and adjust pillows, and administer water, and help with un-needed toilet trips (begrudging the audibly short wee I'd been roused from my slumbers to enable – oh, you weren't fooling anyone with that dribble, Granny).

In the morning, then, who had I been? Had I been horrible, rage-filled, bag-of-coal-off-Santa granddaughter? Or had I been kind, caring, gold-star granddaughter? I think I'd been the latter. I'd been my actions, not my thoughts. And the same thing applies when I want to scream at the small children I love, but smile sweetly; when I haven't had enough sleep and want to tell my inspiring students that they're talking crap, but say 'Interesting. Can someone else offer a counter argument?'; and, contrarily, when I want to call a friend and admit that I was wrong and I'm sorry, but, because I am at least 20 per cent asshole, I don't.

The problem with this conception of identity – that it's actions rather than essence – is that it leaves the idea of the self unstable. I might be shouty, screamy Emer one minute, and all-singing, all-dancing Emer the next. So, who am I? What is identity? Are you your last word, your last action? The idea that identity is constantly in flux clashes with how we experience ourselves: that is, as more or less the same person from day to day. Sure, you might act out of character now and then. Your friends might say 'she hasn't been herself lately.' But you still *have* a character to act out of: you're still you.

Once I was fighting with my ex-boyfriend because he said something completely horrible. I Skyped my cousin Sarah, all tears, wondering if I should break up with someone capable of talking to me like that (I know that sounds extreme, but it was *really* horrible). And Sarah said (because Sarah is wise as a whole barnful of owls at a wisdom convention) that a person is not your last conversation with them: a person is all the conversations you've ever had with them.

Sarah said that my boyfriend was not this one bad thing, but all the wonderful things he had been in all the years that I had known him PLUS this one bad thing. If bad things continued to accrue, then I'd have to change my understanding of his identity, but this one act shouldn't be enough to completely change my perception of the person I knew. It was out of character. And she was right – he was an incredible partner, a person who enriched my life in ways I can't quantify, and his very occasional super-twattery is not what I think of when I think of who he is. So I suppose what I'm trying to say is that we're not just acts, but acts over time.

Simone de Beauvoir famously says: 'one is not born, but, rather, *becomes* woman.'[44] And she means, I believe, that our gender identities are acts over time. A contemporary writer who has developed this idea in exciting ways is Judith Butler. Thinking about gender as a series of acts or performances does have its limitations, because when we think of acting and performance, we think of something intentionally constructed, something intentionally not 'real'. Most actors know they're acting – they don't think their performances represent their identities. So can thinking of gender as performance ever be more than just a metaphor?

Butler moves beyond metaphor, by saying that gender identity is not performance, but what she calls 'performative'. Performative gender is dramatic, but, unlike a stage play, it's not a representation. Where the word performance implies that there is a 'real', 'true' actor underneath the character, performativity implies that there is no 'real', 'true' identity underneath our actions. The word 'performativity' tells us that we perform our identities into being, by repeating acts and behaviours over time.[45]

These behaviours begin to feel 'like us'. Think, for example, of the way you dance (presuming you dance). It has been conditioned by expectations for your gender, by the music you listen to, by the kinds of friends you have, by the dancing you've seen on television and on film, perhaps by your family, perhaps by your education. But it is still you – no one else lets loose on the dancefloor in quite the same way and, like my cross-dressing incarnation in Chapter Three, you have to work quite hard against what has come to feel natural in order to dance differently.

Unlike actors on a stage, we believe in our performances: we believe that they represent who we are. As indeed they do; our performative identities are unique, authentic and individual. However, it's also important to remember that performative gender is conditioned through social sanction (good girl!) and social taboo (that's not very ladylike, is it?) in very powerful and lasting ways.

Butler doesn't deny that biological sex exists (some people accuse her of this), but she thinks it's important to examine the processes through which biological sex is coded and given meaning within societies. She also doesn't claim that we're all automatons, performing according to some rigid script, with no ability to think, choose, or act for ourselves. Rather, she thinks that our bodies are conditioned to perform in certain ways, but we can 'do' our bodies differently.

Butler is working philosophically against the prevalent idea that gender is some kind of natural psychological or spiritual expression of biological sex (there are parallels with Bem, who, as we saw in Chapter Three, used a more scientific set of tools to challenge the once-dominant idea that psychological and social wellbeing is related to the degree to which your gender identity 'matches' your biological sex). For Butler, gender isn't *expressed* through acts, but *created* through acts. And, in an optimistic and positive vein, she sees the fact that society is so quick to condemn people who don't 'do' their gender right as proof that, on some level, people are aware that gender is a social rather than a natural construct.

CULTURAL CODES, CULTURAL COSTUMES

Based on biological sex, the doctor or midwife shouts 'It's a girl!' and from the moment they do so the new human is treated in ways that teach her to perform her gender appropriately.[46] Gendered acts are repeated over time, and become part of the child's identity. One of the characteristics of this process is to create and exaggerate differences between male and female children from an early age. Blue for boys; pink for girls. Long hair for girls; short hair for boys. Trousers, trains, cars for boys; dresses, butterflies, flowers for girls. Boys are not called Anne; girls are not called Barry.

These symbols mean that adults know how to treat children according to gender norms – otherwise little girls might be treated the same as little boys and little boys might be treated the same as little girls, which would be *unthinkable*, obviously. The creation and exaggeration of physical difference between children of different sexes teaches them to act in gendered ways that become part of their identities. It also helps to disguise the spectrum of biological sex, and to create the illusion that an internal, stable gender identity 'naturally' matches the set of chromosomes a child is born with.

Recently, at a party, friends were talking about this coding of boys and girls and how it affects the way we treat small children. A woman I met told a story about a christening she'd been to the week before. She thought the baby was a girl, but because it was dressed neutrally in little blue dungarees (eeeee! – ahem, sorry, but, *little blue dungarees!*)

and a yellow T-shirt, she started to question herself, thinking 'maybe I got it wrong actually – maybe it's a boy.' And she said she found the experience really unsettling, because she was no longer sure how to interact with the baby, and it made her realise that she was treating baby boys and baby girls differently for no reason other than the clothes they wear.

Costume is important. If children are coded and treated differently in the playroom, how can we possibly expect them, as adults, to act as though they are first and foremost human beings who should be treated equally in the boardroom or the kitchen? Costume affects the way adults treat children, and the way adults treat children shapes the people they become. Costume becomes identity; performance becomes reality.

As babies and children, if girls and boys weren't costumed differently, it would be difficult to tell many of them apart, and so they'd probably all be treated much the same. Then puberty kicks in, and secondary sexual characteristics appear. Breasts sprout, balls drop, hair grows in previously bald crevices and men become, on average, bigger than women. So, logically speaking, you'd think this would be a time when we could relax gendered costuming and exaggeration of difference, as other ways to tell whether a person is male or female emerge.

However, at puberty we actually increase the codification, adding gender markers to the trousers, skirts, short hair and ponytails that we've used to gender people since childhood. Adult men smell like pine; adult women smell like flowers. Women apply paint to their faces and nails, while men do not. In ways like these, gendered coding becomes more intense.

As well as tacking further gendered symbols to males and females after secondary sexual characteristics appear, we exaggerate the physical differences that do exist. Men tend to grow more body and facial hair than women (although almost all women also grow body hair and approximately 40 per cent grow facial hair[47]), so we exaggerate this difference by making the female face and body hairless.

Women grow breast tissue, while most men do not, so our society fetishises large breasts (although gynecomastia – a condition where men grow excessive breast tissue, is extremely common, affecting at least 32 per cent and up to 65 per cent of men at some point in their lives[48]). Almost 10,000 women underwent breast enlargement surgery in the UK in 2012.[49] And, as a small-chested woman, I can attest to the nigh on impossibility of finding an unpadded A-cup bra. I ask you: do these mythical devices even exist?

Men, on average, are bigger and taller. Therefore the ideal mediatised male in our society is hulkish, and men try to put on muscle to be considered socially valuable. The ideal mediatised female is waifish; women, in turn, diet in order to be considered socially valuable.

Through this costuming, coding and exaggeration of difference, we continue to disguise the spectrum of biological sex in adulthood and offer symbolic justification for the unequal treatment of men and women. Men – hairy, pine-scented and unadorned – are from Mars; Women – hairless, flower-scented and hung with trinkets – are from Venus. Such different creatures merit different treatment and must play different social and cultural roles. Women, childlike decorative blossoms, clearly cannot run governments and businesses like adult, practical, sturdy men.

WHAT SHOULD YOUR BODY MEAN?

There are some activities that having a male or female body must by necessity exclude you from, like childbirth, sperm production, breastfeeding and certain levels of competitive sport. But, for the most part, there's really very little that one sex can do that the other can't – not changing nappies, climbing mountains, putting up shelves, pole dancing, cooking a nutritious meal for four, fixing a car engine, nor dancing naked in the rain.

While there are physical differences between men and women, cultural developments have radically transformed what these differences must mean. And yet women and men continue to play extremely different social roles. Sandra Bem illustrates the history and tradition behind this paradox by pointing to the fact that although, for the first time in history, very few activities can't be done and done well by men and women alike, in the United States many institutions make it extremely difficult to be both a parent and a career person. And because it's women who get pregnant, and because, traditionally, childcare is women's work, it's women who leave the labour force. For Bem, this is clearly about power, history and tradition, rather than about what women and men are capable of.[50]

There are, of course, still people out there who think that

the reproductive function of women's bodies should exclude them from the public sphere. The technical term for these people is gobshites.

In general, when it comes to thinking about what our different bodies should exclude us from, I like to remember a thought experiment that I learned in the ethics module of my philosophy degree. Imagine you have a society in which half of the people are born with springs on their feet, which enable them to jump really high. And now imagine that, because of this, some spring-foot people design buildings with entrances at a level that you have to have spring feet to reach. They don't bother providing any stairs for the less-than-springy footed. This obviously excludes people without spring feet from certain social spaces and thus limits their opportunities. Fair?

Of course not. And this is why all our buildings need wheelchair ramps. Or – to extend the allegory from disability rights to women's rights – why we need parental leave. People come in different bodies, and those bodies are capable of different things. We need to stop excluding people from the public sphere because of bodily difference.

There is a huge disconnect between what's necessitated by biological sex and the actual gender roles created by our society. Yet many people still try to justify social difference, and – by extension – social disadvantage, by citing biological difference. This is prejudice and nothing more. Male and female roles in our society are not tied in logical ways to the reality of male or female bodies, but to shared sets of beliefs about what it means to exist as a man or as a woman. These beliefs are stereotypical and sexist, and they are at the root of female disadvantage.

One of the problems in trying to challenge and change these 'common sense' beliefs is that most of us have gender identities that are the product of the very ideas and norms that we're critiquing. This means that even the way we experience ourselves as women upholds the gender binary. And so it's crucial that we, as feminists, examine our gender identities, think about where they came from, how we express them through our bodies, and how we can play with gender performativity in the service of equality rather than patriarchy.

CHAPTER SIX:

BODIES ON SHOW

'…feminists must reframe the cultural debate on sexual inequality so that it focuses not on male-female difference but on how androcentric discourses and institutions transform male-female difference into female disadvantage.'

Sandra Bem[51]

BOOB MANIA

Let's talk about tatas. Let's blow about baps, berthas, boulders, bazoombas, badoinkies. What's with boobs? Yes, they are merely lumps of fat and flesh attached to the front of most female and some male torsos. But they are also so sexualised and fetishised that many women pay thousands to have theirs cut open and stuffed with silicon in order to be considered sexually attractive. It's very, very strange.

Boob mania is culturally specific – there are lots of societies in the world where people do not assume that a flash of female nipple necessarily reduces any nearby male to a puddle of warm ejaculate. Women from these societies frequently express surprise that Western men appear to be

GIRLS WILL BE GIRLS

obsessed with breasts. Do men from our culture think that
they are suckling babies? In some societies, other female
body parts – such as the legs – are taboo, while bare chests
are normal. Even within our culture, there are times when
breasts stop being read primarily as bouncy sex balls: when
women are breastfeeding, there's pretty wide acceptance of
the fact that shouting 'phwoar' is bad form.

So let's tear the belief that the Western taboo and resultant
obsession surrounding our bajongas is somehow uncontrol-
lable or based on natural male behaviour into little papery
pieces and throw it to the wind. And let's try to approach
the question 'what's with boobs?' from a different angle.
What kinds of beliefs about and behaviours towards women
does the fetishisation of cha-chas allow?

First of all, boob mania sets up social shame and personal embarrassment around the female body and impedes
women's bodily freedom. Imagine: you're at Claire's party.
It's a hot, close summer night and you've transformed yourself into the proverbial maniac on the dancefloor. Numerous
men in a variety of sizes, shapes, scents and states of hairi-
ness have removed their upper garments and are no longer
concerned about sweat patching their favourite T-shirts.
Yours, on the other hand, is getting ruined, and the damp
circles enthusiastically mushrooming down your ribcage are
most unladylike. But imagine what would happen if you
took your top off too?

Well, depending somewhat on the calibre of partygoers,
out would come the camera phones. BOOBS. Let's show
the internet! The internet needs *more* boobs! And even
though the uploaded pic would contain five naked, sweaty

dancefloor torsos, only one would count as naked, and only one of the sweaty dancers would be the subject of shock and ridicule – you! And then, of course, there would be pictures of you with your dumplings out surrounded by semi-naked men on Instagram, which would be a joy to explain to your Auntie Mary, not to mention to future employers. 'I was hot,' you'd explain, 'I was ruining my T-shirt. Lots of people had their tops off!' But no one believes you: you couldn't possibly have exposed your funbags because you were hot and sweaty; you must have been the main attraction at some kind of Dionysian sex disco.

Before too many camera flashes can go off, a protective friend runs over clutching the summer cardie she brought just in case. She wraps it round your shoulders (which still just want to shimmy shake), and leads you carefully off the dancefloor and towards the site of every important mid-party conversation that has ever taken place – the third step from the top of the stairs. 'Love,' she says, 'I think you've had too much to drink.' 'I've only had two cans of lager!' 'Then why would you take your top off?' she enquires in a tone usually reserved for crying children who have superglued their fingers together. 'Other people had theirs off,' you protest.

Your friend gently explains that there is such a thing as being the wrong kind of maniac on the dancefloor. She is worried about you. She suggests that you both go home. Claire never invites you to a party again. If only you'd kept your gobstoppers under wraps – you'd have made a mess of your T-shirt, sure, but you'd have kept your job, your friends and, if those sweat mushrooms didn't become much bigger, maybe even your pride.

Exposed female breasts must be sexual. We couldn't possibly be getting our hooters out for anything other than 'the lads'. While we've no problem understanding the obvious reason most of the men at a barbecue might have their tops off – that is, physical comfort – women's bodies are so much considered public property that we can't imagine that a woman might be removing layers for any reason other than to titillate. Men's choices around their bodies are for their pleasure; women's choices around their bodies are for everyone else's pleasure.

The taboo surrounding women's breasts also allows their bodies to be commodified and commercialised. That is, it allows people to make money out of women who are willing to break the taboo in a way that confirms that breasts are primarily for horn-dog fun times. Semi-pornographic publications like *Nuts*, *Zoo*, *Loaded* and Page 3 have made hard cash for their (predominantly male) editors, photographers and shareholders through selling pictures of young women whose exposure of their wilsons is not in the name of bodily comfort or freedom, but for the sexual pleasure of men.

So, through the completely nuts but politically loaded taboo on women's breasts, women's bodies become commodities out of which businessmen make money. And, through this process of commercialisation, the taboo is reaffirmed, making it even more difficult for women to have the same bodily freedom as men. The often young and impressionable men buying this material learn that women's bodies are products that they can pay to consume, strengthening a pretty obvious power dynamic.

Aside from making money for men in suits, the taboo on women's breasts allows slut shaming, rape apologism and other sexist attitudes. If the women in the lads' mags are knowingly exposing their melons for the jollies of men, then all females with cleavage on show must be doing so too. If she's got her muffins out, she's probably a slut. If she's not a slut, then why is she dressed like that? Suddenly, simply by failing to sufficiently hide your breasts, you are purposefully communicating that you are wet, wild and mad for a tit-wank.

I think this is particularly a problem for larger-chested women. While I'm not read as all that sexual in a string vest or low-cut top, and feel comfortable wearing clothes like this to class, a woman I know who dresses similarly was once told by a senior male colleague that what she was wearing was inappropriate to teach in, which really upset her. Or, my friend Maev, wearing clothes much on a par with the rest of our female friends on a night out, is subject to frequent comments and sexual innuendo about her big breasts, from women as well as men. What's she supposed to do? Cover up all the time?

We've all heard the 'you should have seen what she was wearing', or 'what does she expect if she dresses like that?' responses to tales of sexual harassment and rape. The taboo on breasts successfully convinces us that women's breasts are so provocative that men cannot possibly come into visual contact with them without losing all reason to the degree that we actually blame women who are attacked for failing to sufficiently hide their bodies.

Boob mania also allows women to be discredited professionally. At my PhD induction, my university offered a course called 'managing your research', in which a woman came in to talk to us about how to successfully navigate the personal and professional squalls of postgraduate life. During this official induction, the instructor actually told the women in the room not to wear anything revealing in professional situations. She illustrated this stellar advice with a tale of a conference she'd attended, where a woman with 'a great figure', got up to present, took off her jacket, only to reveal – gasp – an insufficiently modest top. Well, as you can imagine, at the end of boob-woman's presentation, no one had listened to a word she'd said. They'd all been too fixated on her delectable norks to care about the quality of her research. What a silly titty cow!

If I was running the induction, my advice to the women and men in the room would have been: strive to create a world in which women's bodies are not used to discredit them professionally. The advice offered by my university's graduate school was 'You jiggle, we giggle!'

So what's the answer? Should we all get our puppies out as an act of defiance? Not so simple. Every time I talk about this issue in mixed company, there's an oh-so-clever man who makes the oh-so-witty observation that he fully supports a feminist movement that encourages women to go topless in public! What can he do to help? – hur hur. Where can he donate? – hur hur.

Of course, there are spaces where attempts to dismantle

the sexual taboos surrounding women's breasts are read as they're intended. But, in the age of ubiquitous cameras, these are increasingly few. Burning Man Festival – the fountain of all hippiedom – has traditionally been a site at which the social meanings attached to nakedness, both female and male, have been challenged, and safe spaces created for people to explore bodily inhibitions. And Critical Tits, an all-female topless bike ride, has been a staple of the festival since 1996. The event means different things to different people, but it's basically guided by idea that, en masse, women can shed the inhibitions surrounding their bodies imposed on them by society and can feel free, have fun and be proud of the parts of them usually hidden for propriety's sake. Sounds pretty amazing, right?

In a collection on political performances, the writer and artist Wendy Clupper talks about her experience of the event. The mood preparing for the ride was jubilant: in a spirit of camaraderie and celebration, women painted parts of each other that they usually wouldn't even see. But patriarchy soon reasserted itself. Crowds of men flanked the parade, taking pictures without permission and cat-calling the women with the 'best' hubcaps. Clupper's feelings on her participation are decidedly mixed. On the one hand she still believes the ride gives the women the opportunity to display their bodies by choice, and she believes it keeps the important debates about female bodily freedom alive. On the other hand, she felt objectified and gawped at, and expressed regret that the men exploiting the ride could so undermine its feminist purpose.[52]

Although biological sex is a spectrum and not a binary,

there are people with men's bodies and people with women's bodies. We exaggerate these differences, and then place sexual taboos on the female body, defining female nakedness differently and declaring it inherently erotic and/ or shameful. This is a gendered use of the fact of biological sex: a social use that allows slut shaming, commodification and curtailing of female freedom. You have a body that can only perform sexually – only for others, and not for yourself. Through shared social beliefs, difference has been turned into disadvantage.

THE NEVER-ENDING STORY: OUR ENDURING BEAUTY MYTH

In the last chapter, I suggested that through the coding of male and female bodies we uphold a gender binary. One particularly destructive use of the binary is that it allows us to be convinced that since there's a simple distinction between male and female bodies there's also a 'best', most male body and a 'best', most female body. This is another social use of the fact of biological sex and, like boob mania, it disempowers women.

There's no need for me to describe our society's ideal bodies for you – you know what they look like. Many of you are probably battling, right this moment, to make yours more closely resemble the female edition. And that's completely understandable: the media we consume has been convincing us that there is a correct female body since we were old enough to focus our eyes, and cosmetic industries spend a whole heap of money convincing us that our bodies are flawed, but can be fixed by buying their products.

Think about the bodies you see on TV. While there's definitely a male 'Mr Universe' ideal that we can all recognise from Calvin Klein and Diet Coke ads, and while objectification of men is a problem that is getting worse, causing gym addiction, steroid abuse, disordered eating and all the horrible psychological struggling that goes with thinking your body is wrong, 'ideal' male bodies are not the *only* bodies you see on television. You see fat men, old men, drain-pipe skinny men and everything in between.[53]

But when it comes to women, if your only knowledge of humanity was through the tube, you'd likely believe that female humanity came in only one size and shape. The slight variations on this ideal become talking points – Shakira's hips, J Lo's bum, Kate Moss's small breasts, Christina Hendrick's big ones – even though these aberrations are every bit as common in the general population as the features of the 'ideal' form.

In spite of all the evidence from the world around me telling me incontrovertibly that healthy, beautiful people come in all sizes and shapes, I believed in the mediatised myth of the ideal body. I believed it 'til the point where I was quite ill, and fainting at inconvenient theatrical moments. My friends were fooled too. And, in each other's supportive company, we went to greater and greater lengths to perform ideal femininity. At some point in my mid-twenties, I took a step back from it all and thought, quite simply, 'uh-oh'.

Where once a slick of fake tan before a wedding would have sufficed, now we were UV-ing ourselves on sunbeds.

Where once a Wonderbra would have been cheat enough, I now knew three women who'd had silicon surgically implanted into their chests in the belief that this would boost their self-esteem. When I dared suggest that confidence based on the size of your breasts isn't confidence at all, I was called judgemental. A quick shave in the shower metamorphosed into expensive and painful hair-removal procedures; eye cream magically transformed into botox; and Spanx came out of its chrysalis as beautiful be-wingéd liposuction.

I started thinking about the beauty procedures and products that had seemed normal to me growing up – padded bras, control tights, anti-wrinkle this and that, fake tan, make-up, shaving. Every time my friends and I bought these products we received a free gift at no extra cost: insecurity. We learned that without fake tan our skin was the wrong colour, without padding our breasts were the wrong size, without shaving our legs were unfeminine, and without control tights our tummies were too big. We learned, in short, that our bodies needed fixing. However, the products we used to remedy our flaws were superficial. The real monstrosities still lurked underneath. So was it really any wonder that in our adulthoods we increasingly sought the permanent solutions of UV tanning, laser hair removal and cosmetic surgery?

There is nothing wrong with my body. And, at the risk of sounding like a bad nineties self-help book, if you don't look like the societal ideal, it doesn't mean there's anything wrong with your body. We don't need any of this stuff to be healthy, happy or physically attractive. I am not anti-adornment: I love playing dress-up. But if we think that we'll make our colleagues regurgitate their breakfasts if we turn up to work without make-up, then there's clearly a problem. For all the rhetoric about 'confidence', 'pampering' and 'looking after yourself' that surrounds the eternal regime of feminine beauty, it really just makes us unhealthy, unhappy, and gives us the belief that, underneath it all, we're unattractive.

At the start of the nineties, Naomi Wolf's *The Beauty Myth* appeared, and was an important resource in understanding how this obsession with 'beauty' procedures disempowers women. Firstly, it affects us professionally – if a successful woman is conventionally attractive, she's there because she's pretty; if she's conventionally unattractive, this is used to attack and discredit her. The beauty myth affects women's place in culture – making them first and foremost decorative, and only secondarily heroic or otherwise instrumental. The beauty myth suppresses and commodifies female sexuality. Also, it leaves us hungry, with the psychological depletion that goes with hunger. Finally, it makes pain seem a 'natural' part of being female, and justifies unnecessary violent procedures against the female body. The myth of ideal female beauty has a lot to answer for.[54]

For me, the beauty myth can't be separated from the processes of performing gender that I've been describing throughout this book. From the time we are little children, we receive messages, both implicit and explicit, about what behaviours are appropriate, and we conform to them, knowing that this is what society approves of – what is expected of us. Whether we're scolded for tearing our tights, or praised for wearing a pretty dress, whether we get admiring glances for padding our bras, or disparaging ones for putting on weight, we're constantly learning to repeat the 'correct' feminine acts over time to make our bodies and ourselves into the kinds of women most valued by society.

NAKED AMBITION

The body is evidence: it's proof that we can't be neatly divided into categories of male and female; it's proof that to exist as a woman means more than to exist for male desire; it's proof that there is no standard, no ideal, that the beauty myth is exactly that: a myth.

And so, how do we make ourselves see this proof? How do we become conscious and critical of the performative behaviours that feel so natural?

Some gendered counter-performances are too dangerous or difficult. I'm not going to take my top off at a sweaty house party: it would endanger me professionally and, due to social reactions, perhaps psychologically too. The taboo on my breasts is too powerful, and is held in place by a symbolic system that makes me a sexual object at the very moment I refuse to be one.

But there are gentle ways to start dismantling taboos on female nakedness. We can start with ourselves. You know when you get out of the shower, dry yourself, then immediately tuck the towel into a little mini-dress that hides your breasts and upper thighs? Why do we always do that? Try tucking it around your waist like a boy. Doesn't that feel weird? Why does it feel weird? Oh, yes, that's right – because we must hide our breasts at all times, even from ourselves. They're so sexual that if we caught sight of ourselves we'd probably just spend all day jiggling them in front of the mirror and masturbating.

Or, you know when you get to your room and you go straight from a towel into clothes. Why not hang out naked for a while? Read. Work. Get used to your naked self. Your body isn't something shameful to be hidden all the time, but something unique to live in and love.

Comfortable naked in your bedroom? Might you dare to hit a nudist beach next summer? They're less crowded than the main drag. Enjoying the nudist beach? How about a mass naked bike ride – most big cities have them. Be creative, be as brave as feels right for you, and help to create a climate in which female nakedness means bodily freedom instead of commodification or objectification.

BEAUTY'S NO BEAST

Challenging the beauty myth should, in theory, be easier than challenging boob mania. No one shouts, 'nice skin tone, sexy!' if you leave the house without make-up. But there's pleasure and even some power to be gained from costuming and comporting yourself in line with our society's ideal of femininity. In terms of agency, it's perfectly reasonable for individuals to want to be considered attractive and to want to feel confident about their appearance.

Yet, stepping back from agency and looking to structure,

it's also reasonable to point out that when we conform to beauty ideals, we exaggerate differences between men and women, disguise the spectrums of sex and gender, and allow our bodies and our behaviours to be policed and controlled. Our complacency allows the beauty industry to become increasingly exploitative, selling intense and invasive products and procedures to ever-younger girls, until it reaches the point where normal women like you and I feel we need cosmetic surgery in order to be confident.

This isn't a popular idea to highlight – that our complicity in the system, and the power or pleasure that we gain from it – is part of the problem. But it does need to be said.

The idea is uncomfortable because it makes many of us feel as though we're being judged for our choices and for the pleasure we get from performing our genders. But broaching the problem shouldn't be read as judgement of women's choices nor as anti-pleasure. Quite the opposite: it should be read as an attempt to understand women's choices in meaningful ways and to change elements of society that coerce us into beauty procedures. Ultimately, this kind of questioning will allow for more choice and more freedom, not less.

I also hope that it'll lead to more pleasure. If our decisions to modify our bodies are based on freedom of choice rather than the belief that we're ugly or socially unacceptable without beauty products, then surely we'll experience pleasure from both our modified and unmodified bodies, as well as from a wider range of gender expressions. Pleasure by three!

To dig a little deeper into structure, agency and the beauty myth, let's think through the example of cosmetic surgery. In terms of structure, we should recognise a cultural system that places a sexual taboo on breasts in order to commodify and control the female body; we should recognise that we live in a society that values women in terms of physical appearances; we should know that 90 per cent of cosmetic surgeries are carried out on women,[55] and acknowledge the sexist attitudes to female bodies that underlie this fact.

However, in terms of agency, we must also be able to see that only a minority of women raised in this structure choose plastic surgery, and to listen to the voices of women who say that it is their choice. Feminist theorist Kathy Davis, after in-depth interviews with women from a variety of backgrounds who opted for cosmetic surgery, says that, far from being enthusiastic defenders of the beauty industry, most women she spoke to very consciously faced a feminist dilemma: they knew that they felt sub-standard because of an arbitrary, unfair and illogical 'beauty' standard, but they wanted to eliminate suffering based on this standard that they felt had gone beyond what they should have to endure. If the beauty standard was out of their control, cosmetic surgery allowed them to take back some power.[56]

Davis found that for many of the women she interviewed, cosmetic surgery felt like the lesser of two evils. I can relate – I hate the imperative to be thin at the same time that sometimes I strive to be thin. It's an energy-sucking internal dilemma, but at times when I'm stressed out and lacking confidence I crave the boost and social approval that a smaller pair of jeans and a flatter tummy buys me.

Davis says: 'The act of having cosmetic surgery involves

going along with the dictates of the beauty system, but also refusal to suffer beyond a certain point.'[57] I get this. Deeply. You feel ashamed of your body and you want that feeling to stop. You can recognise that a messed-up social system has made you ashamed, but you choose a course of action that will make you feel better. You haven't changed the structure, but you've given yourself some agency within it.

It's infinitely harder to change the system, of course, and the enormity of trying to do so can make you feel powerless. But rejecting body policing and body conformity doesn't have to mean that we stop gaining pleasure from performing our gender identities. By consciously manipulating the ways in which our bodies signify, we can still dress up and feel beautiful and confident without reinforcing the beauty myth. More beautiful. More confident.

One of the untruths about feminism is that it's anti-fashion and anti-adornment. While my feminism leads me to reject many grooming practices and embrace androgynous gender bending, I know plenty of feminists whose body non-conformity is extremely modified, yet still provocative and political: tats, piercings, blue hair and home-printed tees are completely par for the funky feminist course.

I also know many excellent feminists who love mainstream fashion. In *Bust,* a feminist zine from the nineties, I once read an article in which the writer defended her love of women's magazines by saying that they proved fashion was a performance that girls put on especially for other girls. And while I don't think this defence of fashion magazines would stand up to scrutiny for very long,[58] there's something in it that I really like. As a fusty academic, I might describe that something as women's awareness of how we are likely to be read, of how to use our bodies to manipulate cultural codes and send out messages.

I think there's huge feminist potential in fashion. Through it, we can create visual and sensual expressions of femininity that play with gender norms and celebrate diverse forms of beauty instead of the white, thin, able-bodied, middle-class kind that so many of us aspire to (or struggle to stop aspiring to). Fashion is an art: it can be political. If Keats was right and truth is beauty, then our beautiful, diverse bodies – male, female, adorned, unadorned, black, white, short, tall, skinny, fat, disabled, abled and all the wonderful variations in between – show the truth that there is no 'correct' gender expression. If beauty is anything, surely it's not uniformity.

Feminism isn't anti-fashion or anti-modification, but it does hold the beauty industry and our relationships with it under the spotlight – as well it should. Thinking about the ways we costume and code ourselves tells us something about what it means to be female in our society. And when I think deeply about this issue, I find that I'm opposed to coerced conformity in relation to my body: I'm opposed to the kind of fashion that strengthens an oppressive ideal of female beauty and that upholds a binary gender system. But I'm certainly not opposed to beauty. The challenge, then, is to create alternatives.

Bell Hooks writes passionately about the need for fashion in feminism. She regrets that patriarchal ideals overwhelmingly inform beauty in our society and says that, 'until feminists go back to the beauty industry, go back to fashion and create an ongoing, sustained revolution, we will not be free. We will not know how to love our bodies as ourselves.'[59]

So what will beautiful revolutionary feminists look like? I imagine that the answer to that question is as varied as we are ourselves. Feminism, like fashion, should be about choice. In the introduction, I talked briefly about Artistotle's ethical theory of happiness: as thinking beings we need to consider how best to act in order to be fulfilled, but the answer isn't going to be the same for everyone. When we think about the symbolism of our gendered costumes and performances and about the kinds of beliefs about female behaviour that we're upholding, we'll each come to our own conclusion as to how best to be beautiful.

If, on consideration of your gendered beauty practices, you find yourself unable to work out whether you're doing things out of personal choice or out of coercion, maybe try performing differently for a while. In ways that feel safe and healthy for you, explore your emotional and psychological relationship with fashion and adornment: be confident; be creative; and enjoy a brand of beauty that no one can sell you.

CHAPTER SEVEN:

OH HAIR LAIR DAHLING!

(Say the title of this chapter aloud.
Oh hair lair to you too.)

*'... Women's body hair is seen as, apparently, either
too ridiculous and trivial – or too monstrous – to be
discussed at all. In this sense, women's body hair is
truly configured as a taboo: something not to be seen
or mentioned; prohibited and circumscribed by the
rules of avoidance; surrounded by shame, disgust and
censure.'*

Karín Lesnik-Oberstein[60]

GET YOUR PITS OUT

There are lights and cameras and I'm so nervous that my
face is twitching. I'm on a national breakfast TV show called
This Morning, and I've been invited so that, ostensibly, I
can talk about female body hair. It is becoming increasingly
apparent, however, that I've actually been invited so that
everyone can have a gawp at the crazy lady and her mewl-
ing underarm beasts.

They've put a beautician called Michelle Devine on the

couch beside me, because they want us to fight. Like a good feminazi, I'm supposed to tell everyone not to shave because feminism. And, like a good bottle blonde, Michelle is supposed to tell everyone that they must shave because ewwww. Michelle is an intelligent, empathetic, modest single mum who has her own business running makeover parties for little girls. Our gender politics are obviously different, but she's great. We talk about our preferences and the pressures on young girls to conform to 'beauty' standards. All the same, the station offers its viewers a 'who do you agree with?' poll, which doesn't make sense, because we're not even disagreeing (but maybe I'm just bitter because Michelle won by loads).

I'm getting an easy ride when, by rights, I need to be taught a lesson in appropriate feminine behaviour. Easy rides are not good television. The host, Eamonn Holmes, starts asking me why I'm wearing boots. I can't really answer: 'Well, due to my destructive and all-consuming eight-year education habit, I have no money for anything other than food, booze and rent. I own four pairs of shoes, so it was these babies, stinky Reebok classics, even stinkier Dunlop sandals or tarty stilettos.' Then Eamonn informs me that the viewers don't believe I have body hair at all. So I wave my hands around in the air singing 'Get Your Pits Out For The Lads!' Take that doubters: I got underarm bush like Care Bears got clouds.

My sparkling television debut was all over in ten minutes, and I breathed a little sigh of relief as I made my way to the taxi the station had hired to take me to work. Then my phone started ringing. It was the media. It was the entire media. The media wanted to ask me urgent questions about my hairy armpits. For some reason, 'Are they real?' was a particular favourite. The media wanted insider information on the state of my bikini line, and it wanted it now. I don't know how the media got my number, but it did, and it was not shy about using it.

I answered the first few enquiries, but everything was a bit confusing so I stopped. When I got into work I had to take the minutes of a team meeting, so I put my phone on silent. Afterwards, I had about twenty missed calls from numbers I didn't know, and everyone had left a voicemail. MEDIA. I checked my public e-mail address. MEDIA. I checked my private e-mail address. MEDIA. How did they even get my private e-mail address? MEDIA. Karen, one of my incredible PhD supervisors, called: 'Hey Miss Media Sensation. They're calling me to get to you now. Should I give out your number?' MEDIA. The university press office called my colleague's extension (I was but a lowly part-time research assistant and had no extension of my own). Did I want to talk to the BBC? MEDIA. The department administrator called a different colleague's extension. She had a journalist on hold. What should she tell him? MEDIA.

Noticing me staring blankly at my computer screen, my other incredible PhD supervisor and boss, Helen, told me that I looked a bit frazzled and asked if I wanted to go home. I met my then-boyfriend and some friends of ours for a drink while my phone rang silently in my bag, my inbox filled up, and, unbeknownst to me, the internet regurgitated smiling pictures of a neatly dressed, wee brunette with her hands happily in the air, armpits a-growling. By morning, the interview requests were coming from continental Europe, South America, Scandinavia, New Zealand, Australia, East Asia and the dwarf planet Pluto. I was faced with numerous dilemmas. Should I, for example, strip for the *Sunday Sport*?

Confucius say: If hairy woman do not want to be at centre of bizarre media circus, hairy woman should not go on national TV and wave hands around in air singing 'Get Your Pits Out For The Lads'. And fair enough, friend Confucius, you have yourself a point, but I suppose I just hadn't really thought it would be that big a deal. Which was stupid really, because I'd been living in my hairy body for eighteen months at that stage, and I knew first hand what a big deal it had been for me and for many of my loved ones. All the same, I certainly wasn't prepared to become what my friends mockingly dubbed: 'the international face of female body hair'.

THERE'S SOMETHING IN THE HAIR

Let's take a little rewind. How does one become the international face of female body hair? Well, first one must stop shaving. I hope that some of the reasons I stopped shaving are apparent from this book so far. I'd been doing a lot of thinking about the ways girls and women are conditioned into strictly female females. I'd been considering performativity – how the actions we perform over time constitute our identities – and the radical potential of performing differently. I'd become more aware of and sensitive to the ways that differences between male and female bodies are exaggerated; to the ways in which female bodies, in particular, are commodified; and to the destructiveness of the beauty ideals that are such a large part of these gendered processes.

Body hair seemed a particularly potent symbol of the way in which we teach girl children that the changes their bodies go through at puberty are shameful. I wanted to perform differently. I wanted to create a different world for my (hypothetical but adorable) children. But what finally convinced me to ditch the razor?

There was a trigger. Well, actually, at the risk of sounding trigger happy, three triggers. Trigger number one was tugged when I was living in Dublin, circa 2008. It was nearing the end of Ireland's economic boom and people had more money than sense. A new waxing place had opened off Grafton Street, charging 50 euro for a bare arse. Loads of my friends started getting Brazilians and Hollywoods and raving about how great their new porny vaginas were – how much their boyfriends liked them, how lovely and smooth they felt. So I booked in, because I felt like I should.

My mum called and I told her about the appointment. She said: 'Why in God's name would you do that?' And I said, 'Everyone else is doing it.' And she said, 'Tell me, if everyone else jumped off a cliff would you jump too?' And thus, beaten by the same logic my mother has been beating me with since I was five, I called the salon and cancelled. I felt immediately better and realised that I hadn't wanted a Brazilian wax at all. At base, I didn't think there was anything wrong with having pubic hair. But, suddenly, a significant number of my friends were talking about it as if it was disgusting. I'd just felt under pressure.

Just a little while later came trigger number two. I read a news story about Dublin salons offering waxing treatments to eleven- and twelve-year-old girls in the belief that ripping out their 'virgin hair' would mean they wouldn't grow as much during puberty, placing them steadily on the road to the requisite smooth flesh of female adulthood. 'It's about training girls in good grooming,' said a beautician offering the treatments.

And I got angry. Because, first, it's bullshit. You can't stop girls growing hair during puberty by waxing them as children. People grow body hair during puberty. That's what happens. There's nothing wrong with it. And, second, surely the only time you should be painfully tearing hair from the limb of a child is when you're changing the plaster on her scabby knee. I was already feeling resentful that suddenly my pubic hair, previously not a huge drain on my mental resources, was now something of which I was increasingly ashamed. And this story made me feel how wrong it is that we begin inculcating little girls with body hatred at such a young age.

I saw the excellent comedian Kate Smurthwaite perform once. She doesn't shave, and she explained why. She was in the women's showers after swimming, when two little girls ran into the changing room, pointed at her pubic hair, started giggling, and ran out again. Kate, of a generation confident of the normalcy of bush, shrugged and thought to herself 'they'll grow the same thing soon.' But then she thought about how they'd also grow leg and armpit hair. So she stopped shaving.

My hairy epiphany was kind of similar. I was uncomfortable with Brazilians and virgin waxing, as though the whole hairless female norm was being taken too far. But then, how could I be angry, when I was participating in it? At the end of the day, what's the difference between buying a pack of razors for your twelve-year-old and booking her in for a wax? How could I try to claim that my pubic hair was feminine and acceptable, when I was so ashamed of the hair on my legs or under my arms?

Hair became a symbol of all the crap about gender, femininity and what's normal that we just accept as common sense when it's clearly misogynistic. Body hair became a symbol of the extent to which the pressure on us to modify our bodies – merely to be considered appropriately feminine – was getting so much more extreme.

Yet I stayed shaven. Experiments in elective baldness and cross-dressing notwithstanding, I was still at a stage in my life where my adherence to a feminine standard was a big part of my confidence and identity. But the seed had been sown. The more I thought about the reasons commonly given for mandatory female neck-down hairlessness, the more unconvincing they seemed.

I'd been taught that female body hair was unhygienic and dirty. But the hygiene argument held water like a brick wall holds conversations. Hygiene is about keeping your body clean and healthy. The hair that grows on women's legs is no less hygienic than the hair that grows on men's legs. To claim that body hair is unhygienic is to claim that most men in our society are unhealthily bacteria-ridden at all times.

Our leg hair is not caked in excrement, nor are our armpits harbouring deadly viruses. If hygiene is our main concern, we should be shaving our heads, as head hair carries most of the chemical and bacterial debris from your daily life. Or you could chop off your hands: those things are really germy (admittedly, this might be a bit inconvenient). There's nothing unclean about female body hair. Whatever the reason women are expected to remove it, it has nothing to do with health or hygiene.

I'd been taught that body hair makes women sweat and smell. I began to wonder how the folks who authoritatively offered up this logic came across their expertise, since most of them had never even met (let alone smelt) a woman with hairy armpits. Also, I wasn't sure how it could be used to justify the removal of leg hair. I was unable to find any scholarly studies linking body hair with increased sweating or smell (it's amazing what you can find the time to research when you're supposed to be writing your Master's thesis).

But, ignoring those objections, even if body hair was linked to increased body odour and sweat, why must it be the role of a woman to erase all olfactory evidence of her presence on the planet? If, for argument's sake, body hair makes people smell, why are male body odours acceptable while female body odours are not? Why does so much embarrassment and shame surround women's bodies?

Women are human (a radical feminist idea, I know). They grow hair. They sweat. There's nothing wrong with any of this. What's wrong is the shame that we're conditioned to feel about our normal bodies. It's an assault on our health and happiness.

I'd been taught that body hair is 'unfeminine'. But how could something that happens to most of us at puberty, that marks our sexual maturity, be unfeminine? You might as well argue that breasts are unfeminine. Adult women grow body hair. If we define feminine as 'characteristic of women', then surely body hair should epitomise femininity. This, of course, is a biological argument, out of character for a sociologically-minded person like me. Socially, it is characteristic of women to remove body hair. So, in a social sense, you could say that hairlessness is feminine.

But if we're going with social characteristics of women, we might also suggest that representation in politics is unfeminine. Conformity to socially constructed categories of 'femininity' is not, in itself, a positive end. We wouldn't be able to vote, have careers or own property if the women of the past had made a virtue of adhering to 'feminine' behaviour.

Arbitrarily, the female body must be modified in increasingly extreme ways in order to be considered, not even beautiful, but simply normal. We teach young girls to erase, contain or hide the changes their bodies undergo at puberty by buying and using commercial products. We teach them shame. Their breasts must be hoisted, padded, strapped down, the lust-inducing nipples hidden from view; they must, at all costs, maintain the illusion that their body hair does not exist; their tampons should be disguised as sweets lest boys see them and become privy to the horror of menses.

I could see all this and it made me angry. I knew it was wrong. Yet I wanted to be pretty and feminine and attractive, so I participated in the normative behaviour and I continued to shave. It's what you might call a cognitive dissonance – where you hold two conflicting beliefs at the same time, causing you unconscious psychological distress.

I moved to the UK in late 2008 to start a PhD in theatre studies at the University of London. And I found it felt safer to explore alternative ways of performing gender there – London's a more anonymous place. I went home to Ireland pretty often, stopping in to the east-coast capital on my way out west. And it was when I was on a Dublin visit in late 2010 that the third trigger was pulled good and proper.

I was having a drink with friends, and the female part of the cohort started discussing laser hair removal: the pain; the expense; the half-plucked aesthetic of the results; whether it was worth it. I chipped in: it just seemed a bit extreme, and permanent – like you'd never be able to grow your hair ever again, even if you wanted to. The crowd assembled thought this was a ridiculous comment: why would anyone want to grow their body hair? I pointed out that a good number of people at the table seemed perfectly happy to grow theirs. Again, this was dismissed as the chiming of a cuckoo clock. They were men. It was different. And so, in a spirit of genuine enquiry, I asked the million dollar question: 'What, in fact, is wrong with female body hair?'

Never have I heard a group of such intelligent, socially aware people say such stupid things. 'Boys are just a bit gross.' 'Women don't really have hair anyway.' 'Men are evolutionarily programmed to prefer women without pubes.'

When all semblance of semi-logic was spent, they fell back on 'just 'cause' and 'ewwww'.

The answer people seemed to find the most convincing as to why women should be bald from the neck down was that it 'just looks better' (which isn't really anything more than an extension of the 'ewwww' argument). Women must shave for aesthetic purposes. It's unclear why men are not required to do the same. Perhaps their body hair is naturally more beautiful than women's, flowing in silken curls from 'neath their biceps, waving like Wordsworth's daffodils from their knee-caps, falling frond-like from their penises, inspiring joy in the hearts of all. Or perhaps men are not required to be beautiful in order to be considered masculine or socially valuable.

I suggested that the belief that hairless females look better is a culturally conditioned one. We think that bald female legs equal beautiful female legs because we're not used to seeing beautiful women with leg hair. If we grew up in a society where hair removal was still a choice for women, you'd probably find people who like hairy legs and people who like hairless ones. At this, one of the guys scoffed 'Ha ha, grand so, I guess next time we see ya, ya'll be a gorilla.' And, frustrated that this bunch of lefty, arty, seemingly equality-aware people were completely unable to engage with the conditioning that had taught them to think of the changes female bodies undergo at puberty as disgusting and in need of permanent erasure from our visual culture, I thought: 'I will.' And I was. Gosh but I'm a stubborn mule. Or gorilla. Or whatever.

Being a stubborn mule-gorilla hybrid who believed in

what she was doing didn't make my new grooming regime any easier. I decided that I wanted to hair it up for exactly a year to see what I could learn. I broached the subject with my then-boyfriend. 'So, I'm thinking of growing my body hair.' Silence. 'How would you feel about that?' Silence. More silence. Reluctant reply. 'Honestly, not ecstatic.' Silence. More silence. Silence unending, representing an unspoken battle of wills, which my boyfriend knew he could not win. He sighed. 'If it's something you need to do, I'll be supportive.'

In fairness, he took it better than the time I called to say I'd just shaved my head. When I actually became one with my goat legs, we were both surprised to find that he didn't mind at all. Reconditioning myself, however, was not so easy.

BARBIE VS ELEPHANT

It's the day after my twenty-seventh birthday, and I am being a twat. I know I'm being a twat. My face has turned that weird shade of puce that it turns when I'm either sexually aroused or about to burst into tears (which, come to think of it, must be quite confusing for my lovers). I'm about to cry partly because I'm being such an unforgivable idiot, and partly because of the maxi dress. The beautiful, beautiful maxi dress.

The maxi dress is a testament to the high street, a redemption of our throwaway materialist culture, because if capitalism can create such beauty, can it possibly be bad?

Yes, the maxi dress, with its mix of reds, pinks and purples, refutes Marx. The maxi dress, with its halter neck and gold chain across the otherwise backless back, screams at Plato, 'I am no imitation of an ideal form! I AM THE IDEAL!' My friend Louisa (who works for a cool fashion label) got the maxi dress from store samples for me especial. I could never usually afford anything as lovely as the maxi dress. And, although I tend to think that I look weird in just about everything, I cannot help but note that the maxi dress looks pretty good on me.

But I can't go out wearing it. I can. I can't. Yes I can. No I can't. Yes I can! No. No. I can't. I definitely can't. Oh my God, I'm crying now. I'm supposed to be a feminist. Oh great, feminist guilt. As if regular old woman-guilt weren't enough. Stop crying! You'll get mascara on the dress!

I've been growing my body hair for just under six months at this stage. I expected cute fuzz, but it surprised me with its emphatic voluminousness. If they had prettier eyes, my underarms could do ads for Pantene. If you were going to make a movie of my life, Eeyore could easily be my knee-down body double. I've gotten through the winter pretty easy. My boyfriend got comfortable with his unusually furry bed-mate in jig time; my flatmates Jack, Sophie and Chris got over the 'tugging it for shits and giggles' phase, and were wonderfully supportive (later, Soph would grow hers too); tights, leggings and pretty cardies allowed me to wear much the same stuff I always wore; best yet, I'd been getting increasingly comfortable shedding layers at parties with good friends and around people I loved and trusted.

But spring was sprung – cardigans and leggings were

starting to look odd. And anyways, it would be a crime to wear a cardigan over this dress. The point is that it's backless. The point is that it's halterneck. Feeling villainous, I dig out some light jackets. Nothing looks right. The dress is too perfect to accessorise. It's a glorious day. I'm twenty-seven years old. It's my birthweek. I just want to meet my friends in the pub wearing this beautiful gift. But I'm not brave enough to be that freak with the armpits in the shouty gown.

I don't want to be looked at. I feel ashamed of my body. I know this feeling – this feeling and I are old friends. When I was recovering from anorexia, I felt like this pretty much every morning before I left the house. Back then, the feeling sparked a battle between the Barbie on my right shoulder, who giggled, 'you'd feel so much better if you went on a diet!' and the elephant on my left, who trumpeted, 'the problem is not your body – it's the way you feel about your body.'

It's exactly the same now. Barbie is tittering 'just shave your little pitty wits until they're nice and plastic smooth, like me!'; Nelly is trumpeting 'don't capitulate to the social conditioning that has made you hate your own physicality!' But Barbie has put on a tiny version of the perfect maxi dress and she is sashaying back and forth in front of my eyes, twirling and simpering 'Don't you want to wear the pretty dress, Emer? Don't you want to wear the pretty witty dress? Ah la la la la la la la!' As she reaches my left shoulder she swings her luscious blonde locks, knocking poor Nelly from her perch. 'Noooooo...' trumpets Nelly as she falls, 'Don't listen to that stupid plastic bi...'

Why am I doing this to myself? Why don't I just shave? Am I really going to go through the whole summer wearing long sleeves and tights? This is crazy. Distressed, I take a minty green lady-blade from my top drawer and head for the bathroom. I lock the door and take a second to breathe. Then I catch my reflection: colourfully silk-swathed, black mascara-lined, dark armpit aerials a-waving, brandishing a disposable Gillette as though it's a scimitar. And I start to laugh a little. I'm such a dick.

I rescue Nelly from the floor. I clean my face, go back to my room, take off the maxi dress and put on a pair of tights and something with sleeves. Then I pad downstairs to give the dress to Sophie. 'Really?' she says. 'Yeah,' I shrug, 'it doesn't suit me.'

THE CAUTIONARY TALE OF CAPITALISM AND FEMALE BODY HAIR

While, intellectually, I'd had a grasp on the idea of structure and agency since my undergraduate degree, deciding to stop shaving allowed me to really experience the complexity of choice in relation to socially conditioned gendered behaviours for the first time. I never really 'chose' to shave. I started to hack my legs to shreds at about the age of thirteen because shaving signified a leap into womanhood that I was desperately excited to make. In fact, I remember shaving under my arms in the hope that it would make some hair grow. There was never any doubt but that I would spend my entire adult life endeavouring to make my legs and underarms as smooth as a child's. I was a girl, and when I became a woman I would shave because that's what women do.

When I stopped shaving, it was so bloody difficult, so much psychological work every single time I wanted to leave the house in a tank top or skirt, that explaining the removal of body hair in terms of choice became impossible. If it's a choice between being stared and laughed at in public daily or not being stared and laughed at, what choice are you going to make? If it's a choice between feeling normal and comfortable when you go to work, and feeling desperately self-conscious in the knowledge that your co-workers may be whispering about your body hair when you leave the room, what choice is there really? The only reason I made it through the summer of 2011 at all (including an immensely sweaty trip to blistering Japan) was because I kept telling myself that I was only going to be hairy for a year. I'd learn a lot, and it would all be over soon.

Teresa Riordan's book *Inventing Beauty* is about 'beauty entrepreneurs': about the people behind the inventions that have created our modern beauty standards. And, seriously, the 'beauty' treatments women have been told are necessary and/or safe over the years will scare the shit out of you. X-rays to get rid of female facial hair anyone? Oh, no, don't worry, X-rays can be dangerous, but this procedure is perfectly safe! Here: read this groundless pseudo-scientific jargon our unethical lab technicians prepared. Riordan's book is nothing if not a reminder to disbelieve everything that's on the label.[61]

According to Riordan, before World War I virtually no

American woman shaved her legs. By 1964, 98 per cent of women under the age of forty-four did so. Similarly before World War I, underarm hair was not a cosmetic consideration, as fashions up to that point, while often clingy and form revealing, covered up most of a woman's skin.

For Riordan, whose area of interest is the history of inventions and new technologies, the sea-change was the result of a number of factors: female fashions began to reveal more skin; hairless movie stars were thrust into visual culture; the disposable safety razor came on the market; concerted profit-driven advertising campaigns convinced women of the necessity of hairlessness; women's magazines vilified body hair as old fashioned and incompatible with new fashions; and the invention of materials like nylon allowed female flesh to be showcased in novel ways.

Columbia student Kirsten Hansen's Master's thesis offers a history of Western hair removal that comes to many of the same conclusions, but is more outspoken about the capitalist motives underlying the new hairless feminine ideal.[62] Gilette's first razor for women came out in 1915, triggering what Hansen calls 'a relentless advertising campaign on the part of more than a dozen beauty companies, all encouraging women to remove the suddenly "unsightly" body hair and all seeking to make a profit.'

By the time I embarked on my experiment in body hair, hair removal had been a social norm in Western culture for approximately seventy-five years. It had only taken this long to convince almost every person in the Western world that female leg and armpit hair is unnatural, unclean and unfeminine. The female body hair removal industry is worth millions, and countless women are ashamed of and distressed by their body hair.

Hansen says she was inspired to write her thesis because of the zeal with which her friends upheld the hairless ideal. She says:

> ...among my female friends hair removal is considered an annoying, arduous, often painful, but necessary ritual. Most insist on removing leg hair before putting on a skirt or shorts, and balk at the thought of wearing a bathing suit without shaving or waxing the bikini line. Hair removal is considered so essential to some of these women that they refuse to participate in daily activities such as exercising or going on a date if they have not paid proper attention to removing their body hair.

Sound familiar? The capitalist drive to convince women that our body hair is disgusting has been alarmingly successful. But the industry is greedy. It must now convince the world that female pubic hair is dirty too. It must now convince people that male body hair is equally unacceptable. If there's more money to be made from more psychological insecurity, then that's exactly what industry will create.

During my first year of hair, I noticed time and again how much my habitual clothing put me on show. I'd always thought of the fact that women can wear pretty much what-ever they want as a wonderful facet of our liberal society. I'm the first to tell a girl in a mini-skirt that she looks amazing, or to object when others criticise girls in skimpy clothes. I believe in the principle of freedom of clobber: I might not like what someone's wearing, but I'll defend to the death her right to wear it.

But, as my choice of a dress in the morning was now accompanied by a struggle to root out one last clean pair of tights to hide my wild legs and a matching cardigan to hide my ferocious armpits, I began to see how illusory this freedom was. I might have the right to bare my skin, but the parts of me revealed by normatively feminine clothing had to be 'feminised' in order to be considered suitable for display at all. And the feminisation processes were often costly and often time consuming – putting my money and my time in the pocket of the beauty industry. If I failed to comply with the feminisation of the parts on display – if I wore, for example, a cropped top without creating a sufficiently ideal belly or a skirt without creating sufficiently hairless legs – I would have to suffer the twofold unpleasantness of social opprobrium and personal shame. Femininity is not something that women have, but something that women must buy.

My pretty dresses increasingly became jeans and T-shirts. It was just easier. People commented that since I'd stopped shaving I'd become much more butch. It felt like my femininity was out of my control. If I didn't conform to the social norm in one way (hair), I couldn't conform to the social norm in other ways (clothing). My feminine identity, I saw, didn't really belong to me. It was something I had to pay for.

At the same time that a capitalist system teaches us that femininity is something we must purchase, that we are inappropriately gendered if we do not groom ourselves to exaggerate our differences from men, that we are not feminine unless we code ourselves according to an arbitrary conception of femininity, it also convinces us that we are doing the choosing. It took growing my body hair to make me see that – when it came to my body – I was not really choosing at all.

Because of the concerted capitalist drive to convince women of the need for an unnecessary product, my mother and her friends started choosing to shave in the sixties and seventies. For me, there was no choice. What if, for our daughters, Hollywood waxes, cosmetic surgery, sunbeds, botox and all the rest of the products that so many women now pay to consume in the name of femininity, cease to be choices too?

NOT FEELING IN CHARACTER

So I had all the theory. I believed that the prerogative for women to shave was completely arbitrary, that it propped up beliefs about male and female difference as well as attitudes towards the female body that disempowered women in significant ways. I understood that the shame I'd been conditioned to feel in relation to my body made me an ideal little capitalist consumer: I resented this manipulation, and I was determined to feel confident and secure without bowing to social pressures surrounding what acceptable women should look like.

Also, on a personal, sensual level, I quickly grew to like the feel and the look of the fuzz (trust me, no one was more surprised about this than me). It didn't make me smell – if anything it made me smell a bit nicer, I thought. Like, my sweat stayed warm and fresh and human as opposed to the stale tang of sweat on shaved skin. When I was single, I could still get laid. When I had partners, they grew to like my monkey legs – I think mainly because of what monkey legs said about me as a person. My close friends thought I was brave. So, I had the conviction, the support, everything: why was being hairy still so hard?

It took me the whole summer of 2011 to get comfortable with airing my armpits – to wear what I wanted to wear and wave when I wanted to wave. I decided to continue the experiment largely because I didn't feel that I'd achieved what I set out to; I was still incredibly embarrassed and uncomfortable out in public in a skirt. I remember sitting on the Tube on a sweltering day during the summer of 2012 in a pair of jeans, feeling a little pool of sweat collect in the cleft of my ass, staring at the frankly yeti-ish feet and legs of a man opposite, consumed by jealousy.

'He doesn't know how lucky he is,' I thought, 'that he can just sit there in shorts, nice and cool and breezy, not feeling in the least self-conscious, never having even considered the notion that the hair on his legs might be something to be ashamed of, just casually choosing something comfortable and stylish to wear this morning, not having to brace himself for disgusted stares, surreptitious glances and poorly concealed gossipy whispers. There is no sweat gathering in that man's ass crack. It's not fair! I want to be able to do that too.' And then came the self-reproach: 'well, why can't you? What's the point of having hairy legs at all if you're just going to cover up all the time? It's been almost two years now, why do you still feel so self-conscious and embarrassed?'

It was a conundrum and I didn't know what to do. I didn't want to shave, but I was sick of feeling so ashamed. I was beginning to lose hope that I'd ever be comfortable. Why? Was it really just because I wasn't brave enough, or because I was too concerned with what others thought of me? Should I give up – deem my experiment in body hair a partial failure?

I decided to write a letter to the dead French sociologist Pierre Bourdieu.

ASK PIERRE!
(A COLUMN IN WHICH PIERRE BOURDIEU SOLVES ALL YOUR PROBLEMS)

Brixton,
London
Summer 2012

Dear Pierre,
I hope you won't mind me disturbing your dreamless death. I am a big fan, and, also, I fancy you. I know you are dead now and your skin is probably hanging in leathery strips from your decomposing skull, but, for the record, I still would.

But that is not why I'm writing to you. No. I am writing to ask for your advice on something. Two years ago I decided that I was going to stop shaving

(I am a girl). I'd read Judith Butler on the idea that our gender identities are constituted through acts over time, and was excited by the radical potential of starting to perform my gender differently.

But I'm finding that performing differently isn't easy. *Au contraire*, I'm finding that performing differently is tough as gristle. In preparing to screw around with societal gender norms, I anticipated the stares and 'holy shit look over theres' of the world at large, but I didn't expect my own embarrassment and deeply felt sense of social shame. I waste a lot of mental energy bashing myself for not being brave enough, or for caring too much about what other people think.

Why is this? Is it likely to change?

I think you're amazing and I'd very much appreciate your advice. Also, if you are ever reincarnated, please let me know so that I can have sex with you.

Yours sincerely,

Hairy in Hawaii

P.S. I'm not actually in Hawaii

Flat 44 Styx-side Wharf
The Underworld
Time Unending

Chère Belle Pouillée,

Zank you for your letter, repugnantly salacious though I found parts of eet. You are correct zat there has been some disintegration of my previously Euclidean jawline, but, otherwise, immortality is kind to me.

So you want to change ze world? You 'ave seen that many things are not *juste*. Me, I care about ze class system, and want to understand why people who are born poor, stay poor. You, my hairy faux-Hawaiian, care about ze gender equality, and want to understand why women continue to perform their society's idealised version of womanhood, even though it disadvantages them, and even after they see all the messed up sheet behind zat ideal.

I am going to stop writing in ze French accent now, as it is, how you say, exhausting. Please read ze rest of zis letter in a Francophone register regardless. Merci.

You are aware that you are part of a structure. You have been moulded like marzipan: by your family, by your schooling and by the culture in which you live. And now you are in possession of what I have termed the *habitus*.[63] The habitus is the lasting system that each of us has for making sense of and interacting with the social world.

Imagine – you fall from outer space and wake up in a human body. You do not know that you must wear clothes in public at all times (except at the sandy edges of your country, a zone where it is acceptable to be almost naked), that you must defecate in designated defecation zones, pay for food, or approach strangers with due etiquette. You do not know, in short, how to interact with society: you have no habitus. You run around Tesco in the buff, not a Franc to your name, shitting in the freezer aisle, eating Häagen-Dazs with a Captain Birds Eye fish finger, and sniffing strangers as they reach for tins of pineapple.

But you do not do this. You have a habitus. And the habitus enables you to interact with society. It also helps to create the social world. Allow me to illustrate: I know that it is only appropriate to be almost naked at the beach. This rule is part of my habitus. I would not dream of taking my clothes off in a chic brasserie, yet I will happily strip to provocative Speedos at the waterfront. My behaviour, in turn, helps to create a society in which clothes are required when stomping down the street, but are not required when strolling on sand. My behaviour, you understand, strengthens a sense of what is allowable and normal. So the habitus has rules, but it also makes the rules.

The structures of the habitus are lasting: once in place they are very difficult, maybe even impossible, to change. We internalise them and we do not often question them. Everyone we know accepts them too: they are what I call 'doxic', but what you might call 'common sense'.

But this creates a question, no? Why does it appear as though our choices are free? Why, if we all have a habitus, do we not behave like rigid robots, every move predicable according to a set of rules?

The structures of the habitus are lasting, yes, but they also allow us to improvise in response to new knowledge and experiences. Think of a tennis player. She has taken years to learn the rules of the game, and now she plays without really thinking. Her knowledge of tennis has become embodied – she has a feel for the game. Yet, her apparently unpredictable and 'free' action is actually taking place within a set of rules, and if she steps outside the rules she is no longer playing tennis.

Many, even most, of the structures of the habitus are arbitrary. That is, there is no absolute scientific, logical or rational reason why they should be the way they are. On a sunny day, why should I not walk down a busy city street in my Speedos? The sight of my naked body is deemed inoffensive at the beach in Saint-Tropez. Why does it become, suddenly, grotesque and transgressive in Paris? And would it not be wise for me to wear long light layers on the beach at the height of the summer, when so many of us, our skin unused to exposure, are dangerously burned?

Yet, even when we can see that the structures of the habitus are arbitrary, we continue with our 'normal', 'common sense' social behaviours. This is because the structures of the habitus are embodied: they are not simply a system of cold *beliefs* about the best way to behave, but a set of embodied *understandings*. Let us return to the tennis player – her knowledge is in her body as much as it is in her head, and her relationship with the game is emotional. Logically she might be able to see that she is engaged in a futile test of who excels at hitting a small spherical thing across a long low thing with a round flat thing. Yet, if she loses, she becomes upset. She has even been known to throw the round flat thing at the long low thing and burst into tears.

And so, my hairy friend, changing the world is not easy because, even when we know, rationally, that things are not just and they need to change, we will encounter impassioned resistance from the world around us. Some people refuse to see the arbitrariness of the rules they live by. And some, even when they see the arbitrariness, still *feel* those rules so strongly that it doesn't matter what reason says. You cannot simply rid yourself of all the knowledge, both intellectual and embodied, of how normal people are supposed to behave. You might more easily forget how to swim or how to ride a bicycle.

Belle Pouillée, you are highly unlikely to ever be comfortable hairy, in Hawaii or anywhere else. Sorry to have to tell you. I did point all this out to Judith Butler when I was alive.[64] And in her later work she is much less euphoric about the radical potential of performing differently, stressing instead the coercive power of the social structures in which the individual acts.[65]

For my part, I quite like a hairy woman, but then I grew up in Béarn in the seventies. It is part of my habitus. I will certainly let you know if I am ever reincarnated.

Cordialement,

Pierre Bourdieu

I am, of course, ineffably grateful to Pierre Bourdieu for his rare posthumous letter. And I find his theory of the habitus such a useful tool for thinking about the complexity of the interaction between structure and agency. During the 'when will I ever be comfortable doing this?' phase, Bourdieu helped me to cut myself some slack. I was finding being hairy difficult because performing the body differently *is* difficult. You can't just logic yourself out of life-long gendered conditioning overnight. But was zombie Pierre Bourdieu right that I might never manage to wear my leg rugs with ease and comfort at all?

Bourdieu's sociology is often criticised for being overly deterministic – for privileging structure too much over agency. And I can understand that he stresses the durability of the habitus – he's trying to explain why people who are born poor stay poor, and he's doing so in a way that looks at the powerful social forces that reproduce social hierarchies. It beats pinning the blame on the disadvantaged, right?

But there's something unsatisfactory about this too, because relations of dominance *do* change under capitalism. For example, in (most/much) of the Western world: slavery is illegal; homosexuality is legal; hereditary political power has been replaced by democratic political power; women can vote; and disabled people have a legal right to fair access to opportunity.

Okay, people of colour, gay people, the working classes, women and disabled people are still discriminated against, but a lot of activists have worked hard – against societal prejudice and against their own conditioning – to realise these amazing achievements. Bourdieu calls working-class children who manage to excel in an education system designed to privilege the children of the middle classes 'miraculous survivors'. Yet he himself was one of these miraculous survivors, and he gave the world a new way of thinking about class, culture and privilege – he chipped away a bit of the hierarchy.

My experiment in breaking down heavily engrained social conditioning was proving so much more challenging than I'd expected, which seemed to back up Bourdieu's claim that the structures of the habitus, like Duracell bunnies, last and last. Even Judith Butler moved closer to his side. But I had come to think of my body hair as a kind of activism. It confronted people around me with their learned sexism in relation to women's bodies in a visceral way, and at the same time it forced me to deal with my own deeply felt shame.

If, as I argued in the last chapter, female bodies are gendered in disempowering ways, then getting my pits out (thus challenging the beauty myth) was much easier than getting my tits out (thus challenging boob mania), because the gendered meaning associated with it evoked disgust rather than arousal (although, for the record, I could show you some pretty crazy e-mails from fetishists). In short, I believed in body hair. I believed! I wasn't ready to concede defeat to the blade.

HAIR NO EVIL

I did what writers do: I scribbled down all my adventures in furry womanhood, sharing what I'd learned over eighteen months of re-afforestation, and trying to be as honest about the pleasures and pitfalls of the whole thing as possible. And I asked *The Vagenda* to publish it. They did, and it went viral.

That's how I ended up on daytime television singing 'Get Your Pits Out For The Lads'. That's how I ended up all over the TV and radio, my underarm pets preened by the world tabloid press. I'd wanted to say 'Hair is normal. Hair is nice. Deciding to grow it can be a bit of a challenge, but it's okay really. So, if you want to: go for it!' But the reaction I got was so completely out of proportion to this message that it made me see how deeply engrained body policing really is.

It also showed me that asking people to de-naturalise their learned sexism can create anger. One guy sent me an e-mail saying something like 'you have fans', and providing a link. When I clicked, there was a forum with pictures of me and a group of men discussing them in a 'would you?' vein. One of them said he would: from behind. Another suggested chloroforming me, shaving me and, it's implied, raping me. Another posted a picture of the jagged stick with which he would 'do me'. Can you even conceive of a) writing about how you'd like to chloroform a woman or rape her with a jagged stick, and b) actually tracking down that woman's e-mail address to let her know that you'd like to rape her with a jagged stick? Because you don't like her grooming choices. It blows my mind.

Briefly becoming the international face of female body hair taught me that performing your body differently is powerful. Anything capable of generating so much irrational shock and disbelief can't fail to draw attention to the gendered nature of our society. And because the double standard here is so clearly illogical and culturally conditioned, hair provides an excellent starting point for encouraging people to examine the gender binary.

I began to get braver after my brief hairy fame. Partly, this was because I joined the WANG Facebook group. WANG (Women Against Non-Essential Grooming) is a group of body-positive and body non-conformist feminists who reject body policing. It was great to have a smart, supportive forum to discuss the highs and lows of hairy womanhood. When I read about other women doing battle with the body police, it gave me more courage.

After my stint on the telly, lots of women started e-mailing to say that seeing me flash my jungle pits at the world had given *them* courage. That helped too. And, as the months went by, friends said that, because of me, they felt so much more relaxed about their bodies – about hair, make-up, sweating. A few even dispensed with the razors too. So I guess, on a small level, I started feeling like I'd altered the structure of the world around me, challenging the gender binary in small but tangible ways. This, in turn, altered how I felt about my body in public.

In the summer of 2013, I finally got there. I started by dressing in a quite masculine fashion when I had my legs out, as I found this drew less attention. And then I mixed it up, until it reached the point where I was wearing exactly whatever I wanted to wear day to day and feeling comfortable.

At a major international theatre studies conference, among lots of professional contacts, I rocked my legs and pits in a pretty dress and a pair of pretty green wedges. I went to the beach in Brighton with my friends and sunbathed in a bikini. I went to a wedding in a short shouty gown. I felt so happy – I'd done it. Okay, so it took three years, but I felt attractive and confident without having to conform to gender norms that I believed were harmful. I felt like I'd reclaimed my body.

I'm now at the point where I can choose to shave or choose not to. I don't like rules, but, as a rule, I'm more comfortable hairy. I've given a lot of energy to getting here. And I've learned a lot. I've come to believe that while the structures of the habitus are durable, even Energiser bunnies will run out of battery if you're committed to making them bang those little drums. And, when I think about myself giving an academic paper at a conference with my body hair out, I am really proud. Which is silly really, because it's only hair.

CHAPTER EIGHT:

THE LINES

'In the transformation of silence into language and action, it is vitally necessary for each one of us to establish or examine her function in that transformation and to recognize her role as vital within that transformation.

For those of us who write, it is necessary to scrutinize not only the truth of what we speak, but the truth of the language by which we speak it. For others, it is to share and spread also those words that are meaningful to us. But primarily for us all, it is necessary to teach by living and speaking those truths which we believe and know beyond understanding. Because in this way alone can we survive, by taking part in a process of life that is creative and continuing, that is growth.'

Audrey Lorde[66]

BAD SCENES

SCENARIO 1

Colleague: I'm looking for a good dentist near my house.
Me: The dentist I go to is right by you. They're really

professional and highly qualified. They used to be a dental surgery researcher and professor for years at the University of Montréal before setting up their practice. And they're really nice too.

Colleague: He sounds great. What's the address?

SCENARIO 2

Friend: I'd like to have children, but sometimes I'm not sure I have the patience.

Me: Yeah, I have a friend at home in Ireland with two, and I'm always amazed at their patience. The kids just ask question after question, and my friend never seems to get sick of explaining things to them and encouraging them to learn. It's super-human.

Friend: She sounds like a really great mum.

SCENARIO 3

Scientist friend: My boss is Swedish.

Me: Is he?

WHAT'S IN A NAME?

Did you know that after rejections from numerous publishers, Joanne Rowling was advised by her publisher to change her pen name to J.K.? She did. The rest is history. Rowling's publisher knew in 1997 what George Eliot (aka Mary Ann Evans) knew in 1859: people make judgements about the book they're about to read based on the gender of the name on the cover.

When I moved to the UK from Ireland, one of the things that I quite enjoyed was that people weren't familiar with the name Emer, and so, in e-mail exchanges, many weren't sure if I was a girl or a boy. Add to this the fact that my surname has masculine resonances (being most famously associated with the late, great Sir Peter, and also functioning as a slang word for willies) and lots of people made the assumption that the Emer O'Toole e-mailing them was a Mr rather than a Ms. I was acting as the editor of a postgraduate theatre journal at the time and it was difficult not to notice the difference in people's interactions when they thought I was a man. They were more polite and more deferential.

When I got my PhD, the first thing I did (after going on a three-day bender, naturally) was change the title on all my personal accounts and documentation from 'Ms' to 'Dr'. I didn't do this for prestige – I don't particularly like being called Dr O'Toole – I was just sick of having to specify not only that I was female, but that I was either a married female, an unmarried female, or a feminist female. Why do you need to know this about me, bank official? Why can't you just think of me and treat me exactly the same way you would treat any other human being – male, female, married, unmarried?

Names act as signifiers for things like race, class and gender. Because we live in a world in which men and women are thought of and treated differently, if we encounter a female or male name before we meet a person, we unconsciously make assumptions about that person's character – and, because our schemata contain prejudices, these judgements often disadvantage women.

Numerous studies prove this, including one in which science faculties at renowned research institutions were given two identical CVs to assess. Half the scientists received a CV with a female name, and half with a male name. The 'female' applicant was consistently rated as less competent and less hireable, and the scientists were less likely to want to mentor her. The 'male' candidate was offered a significantly higher starting salary.[67] Other studies have shown that biases like this also exist in a variety of industries where names suggest that CVs come from African-Americans.[68]

But it's not just names that work like this. Grammar itself performs. There's a common perception that deeds and words can be separated by a clear boundary: that sticks and stones might break your bones, but names will never hurt you; that saying something is less important than doing something. In ways, this is an offshoot of the concept that there's a clear line between reality and representation that I discussed in Chapter Four. By that logic, there's an objective reality and language operates as a way of representing it.

But for postmodern thinkers, that binary is too simplistic. Language doesn't just represent reality, it also builds reality: mirroring the things that exist, but also creating new possibilities. For me, it's been helpful to stop thinking of deeds and words as two distinctly different categories. Words can be deeds; deeds can be words. And the language we use plays a very important role in upholding the gender binary.

In the fifties, pre-dating Butler, the thinker J.L. Austin famously argued that our language is performative. Gender performativity, you'll remember, means that our gender identities are not stable internal essences, but rather that they exist through the acts we perform over time. Butler, as I've explained, was reacting against the idea that gender is some kind of natural spiritual or psychological offshoot of biological sex. Austin's work on language is a parent to this theory. Reacting against the idea that there's a clear line between deeds and words, he tried to outline the circumstances under which language does not represent a stable 'reality', but rather creates 'reality'. Where words are used not only to say something, but also to do something, Austin says that we're performing 'speech acts'.[69]

In some cases, like standing up in front of a registry full of people and saying 'I do', a speech act is obvious: these words result in a change in your marital status. But, as thinkers who have come after Austin and developed his ideas show, language also performs in more subtle ways – reaffirming the values and the prejudices of our society and contributing hugely to our performative identities.

My former PhD advisor is a woman of colour, and during one of our meetings she gave me back the manuscript of a chapter I'd been working on. She went through the major flaws in my argument and left me to process the smaller notes in my own time. As I went through it, I noticed that she had circled the words 'black' and 'dark' in my writing. Next to the first instance of each, she wrote, simply, 'could you choose another word?' I had written a chapter about race, class and gender in adaptations of Shakespeare. In her characteristic way – where she encouraged me to find answers for myself instead of giving them to me – my advisor made me aware of the fact that I was constantly using the words 'black' and 'dark' as synonyms for 'bad'. I've tried, ever since, to stop doing this.

When I've told white friends and family members about this experience, I've often encountered the response that my advisor was over-sensitive: that it was political correctness gone mad. But I don't think my fellow whiteys have made the effort to put themselves in the shoes of a person of colour who is eternally reading and listening to language in which dark things are bad things. This use of language doesn't represent what materially exists (many of the things I referred to as 'dark' in my chapter – e.g. psychological states, humour, characters' intentions – were not actually lacking light or black in colour); rather it represents the cultural belief that blackness is sinister. And if we bounce off Austin's ideas and consider the way in which speech is also action, then my use of such language reaffirms dubious cultural beliefs.

Back in the early 2000s, I used the word 'gay' interchangeably with 'crap'. I'm really ashamed of this. It was part of the cool speak of my generation: I didn't think about it. Then one day I said it casually in front of my extraordinary friend Brian and he stopped the conversation to say: 'I'm gay, and it hurts me when you use the word like that.' It was brave of him to speak up. I've since managed to eradicate this use of the word from my vocabulary. When I've tried to encourage other people to stop too, I've experienced the same old 'get a sense of humour' attitudes.

When I was a kid we called each other 'spa' and 'mong' as insults. I still catch myself using the word 'retarded' sometimes. I'm trying really hard to stop, because it hurts people. It's difficult because this ableist use of language feels natural and normal and it's out before I even realise what I'm saying. (Update: one year and counting since my last slip.)

Without trying to absolve myself: all of these ways of using language were things I inherited. As a white, hetero-passing, able-bodied person, I didn't stop to think about where my language came from, or about the work it was performing. But, of course, it came from a society that discriminates against black people, queer people and disabled people; its performative effect is to normalise that discrimination.

I probably don't have to tell you that in our linguistic culture male terms are often used as compliments or positive signifiers (man up) while female terms are often used as insults or negative signifiers (don't be such a girl). I have countless examples of times when this has stung, but one stands out.

I was about twenty, and was hanging out with some male friends in a Galway flat. They'd forgotten I was there and were bitching (gendered term in and of itself) about an absent dude. One said, 'he's always whining like a woman.' I instinctively piped up, 'I'm a woman – do I whine?' They all seemed a bit stumped for a second. Then my friend tried to clarify in a way that was less offensive: 'like an *old* woman,

I meant.' I didn't pursue it, even though adding ageism to sexism didn't fill me with joy. It's hard to speak up when you're a woman among men like that. And anyways, I knew the reaction I'd get: I was being over-sensitive; it was political correctness gone mad.

People who aren't directly affected by this kind of language have the luxury to see their speech as empty: they don't understand why people are getting upset. It's not like they've actually *done* anything: words are only words. Sticks and stones, right? *They* wouldn't be offended if 'white' or 'man' or 'hetero' or 'abled' were used as synonyms for bad. And if *they* wouldn't be hurt, then nobody has a right to be.

Nowadays, I'd have a sneery riposte at the ready for anyone who used 'woman' as an insult. And, in ways, these are the easiest parts of the sexist acts we perform through speech to confront – because they're reasonably obvious. If the 'political correctness gone mad' brigade try to shut you up, you can always say something along the lines of, 'gee, thanks for telling me what is and is not offensive to women: I never would have been able to figure it out on my own, using my little woman-brain.' (Or, perhaps, if you're feeling more generous, you could give them a mini lecture on the performativity of language and speech act theory.)

But the gendered nature of language is much deeper than just using feminine terms as insults and masculine ones as praise. The very grammar of our language is based on the idea that we can and should make assumptions about people based on their gender. Without realising it, we're speaking sexist lines all the time. And, sadly, you can't just start insisting that everyone calls you Dr A. Person and communicating only by e-mail in the hope that this will go away.

Think about how you talk about absent friends. When you refer to a female friend, as well as using her name, which probably has a discernible gender, you use 'she' and 'her'. This means that people can discern her sex from your story before they meet her. And, in a patriarchal society, where women are valued less than men, this means that they're already subconsciously colouring her with prejudice.

HE SAID, SHE SAID

Our language tells us something about the shared, 'common sense' beliefs of our society. We have words and grammatical structures for the people, behaviours, objects and attitudes in our day-to-day lives. And the fact that we use different pronouns to talk about men and women indicates that we're a society that feels it's important to distinguish between these two at all times – a society that believes men and women should have different roles.

This is, of course, partially a hangover from a time where the majority of people believed that men and women were practically from different planets. And I find it wonderfully heartening that speech is evolving and presenting solutions to the problem of gendered language as our society is moving towards greater equality.

Some of these solutions are conscious, with feminists suggesting pronouns like 'zi' and 'zer' to take the place of s/he and her/his. While I applaud the effort, I don't think 'zi' and 'zer' are going to work. The reason is that most people don't immediately understand 'zi' or 'zer' and often assume they've misheard you, or ask you to repeat. What's emerged more organically from our society, if clunkily from our grammar, is 'they' and 'their'.[70]

Lots of us quite naturally use 'they' now when we don't want to specify the gender of a third party. Mostly, this is used when it's a hypothetical third party. Like: 'why would someone come to the library if they wanted to talk all day?' (Or: 'is it because they *want* me to kill them?') But it also works when you're trying to avoid mentioning the gender of the person you're talking about.

I used to do this for all the wrong reasons. Back when I was nineteen and had my first same-sex romance, I would use 'they' when I was talking about her so that I wouldn't have to deal with questions about my sexuality. This was great for me because I didn't have to tell lies. However, because I passed for hetero, people would assume I was talking about a man, so my use of 'they' wasn't an effective speech act in terms of performing political work.

I used 'they' in a *Guardian* piece on internet dating a while back. Many of the commenters took my article as an attack on the habits of men on dating sites, even though I distinctly specified that I was talking about the habits of men and women. Even when you consciously use your language to perform political actions, it doesn't always work. People's schemata fill in the blanks you've intentionally left, often in ways that uphold the gender binary.

This said, it's really promising that 'they' is emerging as a response to the need for a gender-neutral third person pronoun in the first place. It's a big step forward from when I was in school. I was instructed to use 'he' and was told that the female connotation would simply be understood. This never felt right – 'he' is clearly not gender neutral.

Later, when I was doing my undergrad, I was warned against using 'they' for the third person in academic essays, as it is, technically, ungrammatical (because you're making a plural pronoun agree with a singular noun). A lecturer told me I could use he, she or s/he. I chose she. Years later, when I started teaching at university, I similarly corrected my students' grammar. But, following a lively class discussion, I decided to stop, and to encourage students who naturally used 'they' to think about the grammar and politics of doing so, and make their own decisions.

The way I look at it is that, to draw on the philosopher Ludwig Wittgenstein, the meaning of a word is its use in language.[71] So if 'they', previously a plural pronoun, is now being commonly used as both a plural pronoun and a singular pronoun, then it has a new meaning. 'They' emerged because it was needed. Our society demanded an ungendered marker for a third party, because, positively, we're recognizing not only that the male pronoun cannot stand for all humanity, but also that a person's gender shouldn't define how we think about them.

'They' is the solution that the English language has organically offered to its problems with gender. The gift is still in embryo, however. The vast majority of the time, in conversation, we specify the gender of a person when we're talking about them. If speech is also action, then it's important to think about the ways in which we're performing when we use gendered pronouns like this. Is each utterance of he or she reaffirming the gender binary of our society? And can these lines be rewritten?

REWRITES

I decided to try using only 'they' to refer to absent people for two weeks. Before I get down to what happened, I'd like to take a minute to discuss the politics of this experiment in gender performativity and language. Some people have preferred pronouns when talking about themselves, and this is particularly important to transgendered people, for whom pronouns can provoke challenging issues around their identities and social expectations.

I'm not – in any way, shape or form – saying that people shouldn't choose a gendered pronoun for themselves and ask others to use it. We still live in a binary gendered society, and specifying a pronoun can be an important tool for trans recognition. But I wanted to experiment with how language might work if we lived in a non-binary gendered society, where referring to the sex/gender of absent people was not expected, nor necessary – a society where the challenging identity issues surrounding language and gender would not exist, for trans people or for anyone else.

Trying to de-gender my language was nearly impossible at first. I had to think about almost every word I said before I said it. On day one, I was talking about what to get my goddaughter for her birthday, and because I referred to her as my goddaughter rather than my godchild, using 'they' didn't make sense. Also, most of my friends have names that allow people to easily discern their gender, and using 'they' didn't make sense in those contexts either.

To get the most out of the experiment, I tried, where possible, to say things like 'my friend', 'my cousin', 'my parent', 'my colleague' or 'my nemesis' rather than actually naming someone. It was a lot to remember, and while it was similar to when I was trying to phase out homophobic, racist and ableist language it was also much harder, because gender seems to be part of almost every conversation we have. It took vigilance and I slipped up a lot, but by the end of a week, using 'they' instead of s/he had become more fluid and manageable.

Here are two strange things that happen when you stop by default referring to the gender of third persons:

First, people gender the character in their heads in accordance with their gender schema, regardless of the fact that you haven't given them any information that justifies doing so. Exercise for you: before reading on, flick back and read **SCENARIO 1** at the beginning of this chapter (pg. 164). Go!

Welcome back! So, as you probably guessed, my dentist is a woman. But the colleague in this anecdote is also a woman. Did you gender her? As one of my proofreaders, she's also asked me to point out that not only is she a woman, but an ardent feminist, who writes and teaches gender theory. I'm not surprised. As **SCENARIO 3** shows, I did exactly the same thing a few months later, presuming that my friend's boss was male – even after spending considerable time and energy on de-gendering my language. We're all sexist in this way – our schemata associate masculinity with authority and achievement. Using language in gender-neutral ways is an eye-opening way to confront this prejudice and start thinking differently.

Incidentally, the phenomenon of my interlocutor responding with masculine pronouns also emerged when I was talking about my head of department, a taxi driver, the dean of graduate studies, an artist friend whose exhibition I attended, my neuroscientist friend and an ex. People responded with feminine pronouns when I referred to my teaching assistant, my friend who's a hairdresser and my friend with two kids.

The second thing that tends to happen is that people get distressed by your failure to provide information about the gender of the person you're talking about, and will flat out ask you. It's extremely odd that we can't process a story about someone without knowing what kind of genitalia they are likely to have, and that we can't imagine a social interaction between two people without knowing whether they're men or women. And it's not just odd – it's sad: it's sad that we can't interact with people as people without applying all sorts of gender stereotypes.

This hit home after a Skype conversation I had with a London friend.

Me: I have to go now – I'm meeting someone for a writing date.
Friend: A romantic writing date?
Me: Nope – a friend. We write together in a coffee shop every week or so.
Friend: Girl or boy?

Me: Boy.
Friend: Is he gay?
Me: No.
Friend: And you spend all that time in coffee shops writing
   together? He probably fancies you rotten.

I regularly meet my friend Abe one-on-one for writing dates.
We sit in coffee shops, talk about our writing projects and,
you know, write. The conversation in which my London
friend requested to know his gender and then suggested
that he liked me romantically or sexually struck me for
two reasons. First, my friend knows that I date men and
women, so knowing that Abe is a man shouldn't really
make a difference as to whether the date was platonic or
not. My friend's comment was based on stereotypes of men
as uninterested in women except as sexual partners, and
also as dishonest in relations with women: the implication
was that Abe was pretending to be my friend so he could
get into my knickers. This stereotype just couldn't be further from my writing bud! My Skype friend is queer and
egalitarian, and their comment was light-hearted, but we all
make assumptions like this.

The second reason the conversation struck me was that
Abe and I had recently had a really open e-mail exchange
about the nature of male/female platonic friendship, in
which we made sure that we were on the same page about
the quality of our relationship. We'd each been experiencing
mild anxiety that the other was thinking in romantic terms
about what we hoped was the foundation of a meaningful
friendship. After the Skype call, I thought about the source

of that anxiety, and, probably because of my language pre-occupation, I found the answer partly in the words we use.

Speaking about each other, telling others about the one-on-one time we spend together developing closeness and intimacy, we use language that constantly reminds the listener and speaker of Abe's masculinity and my femininity. The emphasis on our gender difference over-rides all the things we have in common (obsessions with Doris Lessing, sci-fi habits, guilt over non-vegetarianism, penchants for soft-voiced indie kids singing deceptively depressing lyrics) and means that, in language, we're a man and a woman before we are two people. And I suppose it struck me as particularly bizarre in the case of Abe and I, because he's not a terribly masculine man and I'm not a terribly feminine woman; if anything, it feels like we should share a gender pronoun, not be linguistically placed on opposite ends of a spectrum.

When we're hanging out, Abe and I are 'you' and 'you', but when we're apart, we're 'he' and 'she'. This is what the world hears when we speak about each other; we know this, and we bring the knowledge back into our interactions. It's no wonder that male/female friendship can require so much communication – the very words we use set us up for failure.

SPEAKING TRUTH TO POWER

My attempt to de-gender my speech, like so many of my experiments, is turning into a longer personal project, and into a much deeper awareness of the way language performs and the ways it can perform differently.

I believe that humans are people first, and that their sex or gender is incidental to their personality; yet the words and grammar I've used all my life argue the opposite. This is why rewriting the lines we speak is such a crucial part of creating a world in which we're liberated from binary gender roles.

Why should we allow language to give information about someone's sex or gender unless to do so is demonstrably necessary? Gender-neutral language confronts people with their prejudices – about, for example, assuming people in positions of power are men, or that parents are women; about, for example, assuming that male interest in women is primarily sexual, or that romantic relationships are always hetero.

Changing the language we use creates possibilities, freedoms, and stops people taking discriminatory world views for granted – if the chairperson of the board is a 'they', then we create a linguistic space in which that chairperson could be female, even if the reality is that men are much more likely to occupy positions of power; if the small child I'm taking care of is 'they', it gives the little one freedom to act outside the gendered behaviours expected of them from a young age; if the person I'm dating is 'they', it stops people from assuming that I'm straight or gay, and creates an array of queer possibilities. (It strikes me that for a straight person to start using this kind of language around their romantic life would be an act of great solidarity.)

Language is personal and political. It shapes us; it shapes the world. Words are deeds: they create expectations; they perform actions. The fact that it's so difficult to become attuned to the gender resonances in our language means that we're doing lots of things with words that we don't really intend. And, if our identities are performative, these unintentional speech acts shape us and stay at the heart of the people we become over time.

Language has both pitfalls and potential. On the one hand it's full of crappy assumptions about gender, sexuality, race, class and ability; on the other it has endless possibilities for creating new expressions, new words and new grammars, for imagining new things into being.

If you're game for this, you might like to start with your writing. Analyse an e-mail, report or story you've written. What gender assumptions are present in the vocabulary and grammar? How might you play with these? Perhaps by finding nouns and pronouns that are inclusive of as many groups of people as possible? Or by using pejorative expressions as complementary instead? (A friend of mine uses gay as a synonym for cool – it's become totally seamless.) Maybe by inventing excellent insults that don't draw on societal prejudices? (Simply add whiskey and friends to make this a delightful group activity.)

You might like to start by becoming more attuned to your speech as action. Whether this is simply being aware of the values present in the words you use, piping up when you encounter sexist and other prejudicial language, or attempting to de-gender the way you speak, your words have so much potential to create change.

My friend Brian – the same who asked me to stop using 'gay' as an insult – is one of the people in my life whose wisdom I deeply respect. Once, I was a total shit to him: I was supposed to stay at his, but scored instead, and didn't call to tell him I wouldn't be home. When I re-appeared the next day, he was angry. His sermon went something like this: 'You said you were coming back. I was worried because I honoured your word. But you didn't, and that devalues your word, both for you and for the people who believe in what you say. *You should be of your word.*'

Who needs Yoda when you have Brian? The language we use is part of our performative identities. It shapes us, and also the world around us. It's not always easy, but, knowing this, we should all try to be of our word.

CHAPTER NINE:

SEX ACTS

'Since sexuality is as much a social fact as it is a human one, it will therefore change its nature according to changes in social conditions. If we could restore the context of the world to the embraces of these shadows then, perhaps, we could utilize their activities to obtain a fresh perception of the world and, in some sense, transform it.'

Angela Carter[72]

[**Sexual Violence Trigger Warning**: the section below contains a moderately graphic account of sex to which I consented becoming violent in ways to which I did not consent and ending in a sex act to which I did not consent. If sexual violence is a trigger for you, please skip to page 187. Also, here, have this massive hug.]

SHIT IN BED

Last summer I was out to dinner with friends: three girls and a guy. My male friend had been on a series of odd internet dates, and had stories to tell about weird sexual encounters. One girl wanted to poo on him. He declined. Another offered him an array of butt plugs. He declined. The trials of vanilla dating in a kinkster world, no? We all laughed. He asked us if we had any funny, sexy dating stories. I volunteered the tale of the worst one-night stand I ever had.

The guy was a friend I'd known for years. We were acting together in a play at the time. I think it was opening night. Anyhow, I was drunk and felt like company, and he had always been sparkly eyed and handsome and fun, so I took him home to my cramped attic room and single bed.

When we were naked he started nipple crippling me – twisting my poor wee anemones as though they were bottle tops he was expecting to come off. I asked him to stop, that my nipples were sensitive. He said sorry. Then two minutes later he started again. I asked him to stop. Again. He looked pissed off. He completely ignored my clit and started stabbing my not-yet-wet vagina with his fingers. I didn't ask him to stop even though it wasn't pleasant.

After approximately a nanosecond of nipple crippling and fanny stabbing, foreplay was over, and he went in for some penetration. I asked him to wait while I got a condom. He said he didn't want to wear one. I said he had to wear one. He said it wouldn't feel good with a condom. I asked which would feel better – sex with a condom or no sex at all? He wore the condom.

When he was inside me, he positioned himself in front of my bedroom mirror and started whacking my thighs and ass with his big palms, all the while staring at himself like this was an audition for a remake of *American Psycho*. Now, I do not mind a little bit of kinky spanking, but this man was walloping me. I asked him to stop. 'Oh, you don't like that either, do ya? What *do* ya like?' he enquired chivalrously, before going back to staring at his sexalicious reflection, partially obscured though it may have been by my annoyingly sensitive breasts and thighs.

Neither of us was having any fun. I had had no foreplay, was not particularly wet, and had spent the first twenty minutes of our sexual encounter being beaten up and chastised for failing to enjoy it. He wasn't having fun because I was a human being with a body and a mind rather than a blow-up sex sheep. I wasn't confident enough or experienced enough to know that it would have been okay to say 'this is awful. Can you please leave now?' I was going to see this through to the end, dammit! (The end being his orgasm, of course.)

We were in doggy, him hammering my increasingly dry vag without much enthusiasm. I wanted it to be over, I'm pretty sure he wanted it to be over, but it just went on and on and on, until the coup de grace. He pulled out, and, with neither word nor warning, thrust full force into my ass. I screamed with pain, grabbed a pillow and curled myself up behind it at the corner of the bed.

'What the fuck is the matter with you?' I politely enquired. 'What's the matter with *you*?' he said. 'What kind of guy needs to be twisting women's nipples and hitting them and buggering them by surprise?' I managed to articulate. 'It's the condom,' he said, 'I'm not going to come if I have to wear this condom.' I informed him in a most ladylike manner, but in words, alas, that my publisher would never print, that I had lost all and any interest in his ability to achieve climax. He seemed baffled by my pillow shield and general outraged demeanour, so I asked him why on earth he thought it would be a good idea to bestow the gift of surprise anal on anyone. 'Other girls like that,' he said, adding: 'I thought you'd be a right little minx, but you are shit in bed.'

Other girls like that. No. No they don't. Bodies are not made that way. Girls can take surprise lube-less anal like porn stars in the same way that men can drive cars like James Bond.

Incidentally, it bled when I shat for about three days afterwards. The play ran for two weeks, and I had to hang out with Mr Happy Slappy Butt Rape for substantial periods of time every day. He still tries to friend me on Facebook occasionally. Decline. I don't hate him. He's not a bad man. I don't think it was fun for him either.

So, I finished telling this story at dinner, with most of the girls nodding along or laughing knowingly at certain bits. Because most of them have also had experiences with men who learned their sexual technique from Cocks Fuck Asses 4. The one man at dinner, however, was shocked. Horrified. Had I reported it? Did I stay friends with this asshole? Why was everyone still just eating dinner and snorting derisively like I was recounting a gently amusing mix-up of shopping bags?

In spite of the fact that the majority of people at the very least ask before trying to recreate scenarios of internet fantasy, the effects of porn are simply part of many modern women's sexual realities. None of the ladies (all hetero except me) at the table were the least bit surprised by my tale. From having men insist on bald pubic mounds, to having their clits ignored and vaginas finger-stabbed, to expecting anuses to function like second vaginas, or fellatio to follow seamlessly from anal (yum!) – they'd all experienced the real-time effects of porn at some level. The performance permeates and even creates men's sexual desires and women's sexual experiences.

SEXUAL PERFORMANCE

The way we experience sex is conditioned by the social world. In Chapter Five I suggested that many of the male and female roles that we consider 'natural' are learned, arbitrary constructions. When it comes to sex, this way of thinking can be counter-intuitive: sex is something animal, instinctual, something that takes place in private, something outside the bounds of normal social rules. Surely the way that we have sex is the same way that humans have been having sex for thousands of years?

Counter-intuitive though it may be, the forms sex takes in a society tell us something fundamental, not about an unchanging or universal human condition, but about the gendered power relations in a given time and place. The sex acts we're performing are often divorced from the reality of our physical and psychological experiences, and increasingly married to representations of sex on our TV and computer screens.

What's the difference between what porn stars do in front of a camera and what two consenting adults do behind closed doors in a candlelit room? Most would say that it's a question of performance. The porn stars are acting. The sex we're watching has been lit, staged, directed and edited. The actors are not responding to their own bodily pleasure and desire, but are following instruction, and enacting a version of sex that is meant to be enjoyed from outside, by those watching it, not from inside, by those experiencing it. Porn is costumed and choreographed; the actors are playing roles. It's not 'real'. Yet the sex that people have in private is costumed and choreographed too.

In Chapter Four, I introduced the postmodern idea that the line between representation and reality is blurred – that the symbols we use to stand for maleness and femaleness are not tied to physical or psychological 'reality', but rather to a shared understanding of what these symbols mean. In an era when so much of our early sexual experience comes from visual media, this is especially true of mediatised sex acts.

The kinds of sex we see performed usually reflect binaries – male/female, dominant/submissive, butch/femme, top/bottom – when it's easy to see that sex is always a spectrum. As I have continued to sing throughout this book, categories of masculinity and femininity are not fixed. Likewise, subs can make the best doms; men can be fucked; femmes can be tops. So if, in spite of this, binary sex acts are persistent cultural symbols for us, let's take some time to consider what this tells us about gender and society.

FETISHISING COSTUME

If women believe that in order to be sexy and feminine they need to diet, dye, depilate, pluck and even plastify, we are all wearing gendered costumes, even when we're naked. Our conception of our own worth as sexual beings is tied into the costume. I know countless women who wouldn't bring a lover home if they hadn't shaved their legs. A friend recently told me that when on holiday with her new boyfriend, she didn't swim in the sea once, because she didn't want him to see her without make-up. I've seen friends crying into their cabbage soup, shedding pounds before a long-distance lover comes to visit. I've caught myself holding my tummy in during cunnilingus.

This is not just in our heads. Men are conditioned to be attracted to a costume of idealised femininity – to lean bodies, gravity-defying breasts, long head hair, no body hair, girly clothing and underwear and a made-up aesthetic. From my experiences of body non-conformity, I believe that many men are attracted primarily to the code, the costume. Sure, lots of guys profess a love of the bare-faced, 'natural' woman, but I was amazed at how many told boy-costumed me that they preferred girls without make-up, then changed from friendly to flirty when *I* changed from a hoody to a dress.

Sure, plenty of men find diverse female bodies attractive. But they, and we, retain a shared cultural understanding of the fact that some female bodies are more valuable than others. I've heard male acquaintances laugh about a colleague with a fat wife. I've also had a relationship with a man who very clearly was not attracted to my (then) boyish body shape. He liked bigger women. (He was into fat-girl porn. Oh, and he once generously offered to pay for me to have a boob job.) But he also liked having a thin, socially valuable girlfriend. Men are as conditioned to be attracted to and/or to value a costume of femininity as women are to associate their attractiveness and worth with wearing it.

On the extreme end of the spectrum, you have men for whom flesh-and-blood women can't compare to the exaggerated costume of female sexiness that they encounter through media and pornography. One friend of mine, let's call her Karen, had a boyfriend in university who had erectile difficulties. She was understanding about this, until it emerged that he spent large portions of every day jacking off to porn. His sexuality had become so entangled in visually consuming virtual sex-bots that he was unable to get it up with a pretty girl who liked him in a darkened room. I feel sorry for Karen; the whole thing knocked her confidence no end. But I also feel sorry for her ex-boyfriend, whose ability to experience sexual intimacy was ruined by porn, which he was probably too young to critically interrogate before starting to use it.

I have another friend, let's call her Mina, whose ex-boyfriend was so addicted to pornography that he had to have it on in the background when they were having sex. She recounts lying underneath him and studying his face as he watched women writhe on screen. It was one of her earliest sexual relationships and it was very damaging for her. In spite of the pain the experience caused her, she remains empathetic about her ex. His homophobic father was scared that he would turn out gay and had been showing him pornographic material since the age of nine.

Many people consume pornography in moderation and their relationship with it doesn't dominate their sex lives. I'm not trying to patronise or vilify all porn makers or porn users. That'd be pretty hypocritical: I use porn sometimes. While there remains an ethical conversation to be had here about the conditions of workers in the sex industry (which is, unfortunately, beyond the scope of this book), it's not vilification to highlight the relationship between media representations of sex and widespread male desire for a specific costume of femininity and for specific sexual acts.

The psychiatrist and psychologist Norman Doidge, who has worked on brain scans of pornography addicts, believes that of all human instincts, sexuality is the most plastic, because it has broken free of its primary evolutionary aim – reproduction. He points out that we know that sexual tastes are not hardwired, because they change from era to era, and also over the course of our individual lives. Because teenage brains are especially plastic, he worries about the effects of porn on the sexualities of today's generation of teenagers, who can access violent pornography so easily.[73]

For Doidge, the ultimate sign that sexual desire needn't be hardwired is the fetishist, 'more attracted to a shoe than to its wearer'. But to this I have to pose the questions: what is the difference between being attracted to a woman's stiletto shoes and wanting to come on her feet; or being attracted to a woman's long hair and make-up and wanting to come on her face; or being attracted to her lingerie-clad, hoisted-up, squeezed-together cleavage and wanting to come on her tits? All of these things represent a fetish – a culturally conditioned attraction to a costume of femininity above and beyond the woman wearing that costume.

CHOREOGRAPHY AND THE CLITORIS

Our visual culture represents a choreography of sex divorced from the body: divorced, in particular from the ways in which most women experience sexual pleasure. As sexually active women watching pornography or Hollywood sex scenes, most of us are aware that mainstream portrayals of sex are caricatured. Based on the sex I'd seen on TV, by the time I lost my virginity I was disappointed to find that being banged by a hard peen did not magically create orgasms. I mean, I really enjoyed sex, but for years I thought there was something wrong with me. So did boyfriends, who'd confusedly ask if I'd come after their stellar athletic efforts.

We need to give some credit to Sigmund Freud for this. Freud theorised that the clitoral orgasm (or what might be more accurately called a glans orgasm) was 'immature', while the properly developed woman would experience vaginal orgasms. This was famously debunked by social scientist Shere Hite's 1976 report, 'A Nationwide Study of Female Sexuality', which was based on over 3,000 women, and found that 70 per cent of respondents never reached orgasm through vaginal intercourse.[74]

Onscreen, female orgasms are the result of a vigorous bangarang, and the external clitoris is all but erased from the equation. This confused artist Sophia Wallace so much that she undertook a project called Cliteracy, which aimed to educate people about our poor maligned detonators. And I'm glad she did because before I found her project and set about making myself cliterate, I was completely ignorant of the size, structure and numerous functions of this incredible organ.

Learning what the clit looks like, where it is and how it functions has made a lot of things about the way that I experience sex more explicable, and has made sex even more enjoyable. Anatomical education for the win! Are you like I was? Do you think the clit is just a funbump, a passion pea, a teeny tiny button of OMG? Would you be surprised to learn that the clitoris is massive, it looks like an alien and it gives your vagina and urethra a hug when it's happy?

Five things you may not know about your clitoris:

1. It is the only human organ that exists solely for pleasure.
2. It is larger than an unerect penis, and is a complex structure with many interacting parts, including muscular and erectile tissue.
3. The part of the clitoris that you can see is called the glans and it's only the tip of the iceberg. Even so, it has approximately 8,000 sensory nerve fibres – twice what's to be found in the head of the penis (not that it's a competition).
4. Underneath the surface you find structures including two corpora cavernosa, two crua and the clitoral bulbs. The cavernosa wrap around the vagina and urethra on either side when erect, while the crua, when excited, engorge the vaginal opening.

5. The anatomy of the clitoris goes a long way towards answering the g-spot/vaginal orgasm question – the vagina itself is not erectile or particularly nerve ending heavy, and vaginal orgasm is most likely the product of stimulating the inner clit through the vaginal walls.

If this is news to you, you're probably thinking: 'What! Why did nobody tell me? This is information about my genitals that I would've been happy to be privy to sooner thank you very much.' Part of the reason so little information about the clitoris is mainstream is because for most of the twentieth century there was hardly any research done on it. Shockingly, the clitoris remains either misrepresented or omitted in much contemporary medical literature, including many of the anatomy textbooks used to train doctors. In spite of the pioneering work of the urologist Helen O'Connell in the nineties and early noughties, the first 3D model of the clitoris wasn't made until 2009. So, to put that in some kind of perspective: modern science authoritatively mapped and made models of the human genome before it adequately described or modelled the clitoris.

Clit ignorance obviously leads to misunderstanding of how female sexual anatomy works, and has affected the way sex is represented, the way it is performed and, most importantly, the way that we, as women, experience it. Okay, why? What's going on? Why has the internal clit been so neglected by medical science, and why does it remain absent or erroneously represented in so many anatomy texts?

After her 1998 study, which used the dissection of cadavers, found that current anatomical descriptions of the

clitoris were inaccurate, and her 2005 study, complement-
ing the use of generous dead people with MRI modelling,
confirmed this, Helen O'Connell stated that: 'The anatomy
of the clitoris has not been stable with time as would be
expected. To a major extent, its study has been dominated by
social factors [...] Some recent anatomy text books omit a
description of the clitoris. By comparison, pages are devoted
to penile anatomy.'[75] So, for O'Connell, social attitudes to
female sexuality have led to a sidelining of research into
this area of anatomy. For a large part of modern medical
history, the female organ of pleasure was either too sinful
or too unimportant to study.[*]

The medical establishment's attitude to female sexual
anatomy is changing only very slowly. In 2009, doctors
Odile Buisson and Pierre Foldès produced the first 3D
sonography of the clitoris. 3D imaging of the clitoris is
important because, due to its complex anatomy, it can't be
represented in a single diagram showing a single plane. Yet
Buisson and Foldès had to fund this research themselves.
Foldès, who has used his research to restore clitoral sensation to victims of female genital mutilation for the first time,

---

[*] In a blog post wittily entitled 'The Lady Vanishes', Robert King, a professor
of psychology at University College Cork, explains that the internal structure of
the clitoris was actually discovered by Fallopia as early as the sixteenth century.
It was 'discovered' and described again in the mid-1800s, and yet again in the
1950s, before O'Connell's research brought it back into the eye of our generation.
King explains the absence or misrepresentation of the clitoris in medical textbooks
and general public ignorance of the size, function and complexity of the organ in
terms of what he calls the 'flowers at midnight theory'. Female sexual function is
understood ideologically as an imperfect copy of male sexual function, so when
what works for the male does not work for the female, people have considered the
female body broken. Says King (rather prettily): 'It is as if I found some flowers at
midnight and concluded that they must be faulty because the petals were closed.'

claims that 'the very existence of an organ of pleasure is denied medically,' and believes that the 'medical literature tells us the truth about our contempt for women.'*

So, representations of female sexual anatomy and, by extension, of female sexual pleasure are ideological. They consist in understandings of the female body that are sexist – understandings that regard female pleasure as sinful, unimportant or secondary to male pleasure. As O'Connell and Buisson and Foldès say, the ignorance surrounding the clitoris is not accidental – it's the product of a society that fails to value people in female bodies, people with female experiences. And, while I've noted that I'm not trying to demonise porn or porn users, it's important to recognise that porn is both a product of this society and a producer of sexual desires, tastes and behaviours.

Let's think about representations of female pleasure in pornography. We've already noted that, as in real life, the clitoris is represented as something secondary, and, even when women are being digitally stimulated, the glans is largely ignored. Much porn represents foreplay for the female as a rapid hand-stabbing of the vagina.

Maybe there are ladies out there who are just crazy about the digging-for-spuds approach to sexy-time warm up, but I think most of us will agree that immediate digital penetration with all the softness and subtlety of a pneumatic drill is not our favourite sexual treat.

Many of the stock manoeuvres in mainstream porn are

---

* Quoted in 'The Internal Clitoris', *Museum of Sex*, 30 Nov 2011. (This excellent blog on the subject also has great images.)

painful or dangerous when replicated in reality. Women with asses of steel take nine inches up the botty (look Mom: no lube!). Tits are squeezed, nipples pegged. Botties are smacked 'til stinging red. Blowjobs appear to be less about male pleasure and more about female displeasure. In the world of porn, it's just not hot unless she's threatening to bring her lunch back up. All the while the women moan with pleasure. They come and come from being banged, and ask for nothing more.

When I raise the relationship between pornographic representation and sexual reality in mixed company, heterosexual guys like to claim that everyone knows that porn is a caricatured, choreographed version of sex, not something to actually try to perform on a real female body. And mostly the girls who sleep with guys disagree, without being vocal as to why. Here's why (and it's not because we're all blindly, prejudicially anti porn): it's because we know. It's because many of us have experienced the effects of pornography through partners who've been unable to differentiate between the performance on screen and the sensations and psychologies of reality. And all the dudes out there who say it doesn't happen because they themselves understand the difference between porn and real-life sex – they're probably not sleeping with dudes.

JUST SAY NO

Why, when men perform the acts they learn from pornographic representation on our bodies, why don't we always say no? Why do we allow these acts to move from representation to reality, to become part of the choreo-graphy of our sex lives? This is a complex question.

No two bodies are exactly alike, and what works on one will not necessarily work on another, so every time with a new partner is a process of finding out what works and what doesn't. This can be amazing. Like 'Oh my God, what are you doing with my clitoral hood, I think I love you, let's get married, no not right now, keep doing what you're doing, don't stop, don't stop, never stooooooooop, okay you can stop now. I don't actually want to get married.' Or it can be awful. Like 'yeah, pulling your penis completely out of my vagina before reinserting it over and over again is simply creating an uncomfortable build up of air. I'm sure it's very visually appealing, which is why you've been staring at our combined genitalia for five minutes. But we're both going to be embarrassed when the inevitable result of compressed fanny gas audibly announces its presence. Just saying.' So at the start, you have to communicate – I like this; I don't like that; what do *you* like?

A 2011 study by Fisher, Moore and Pittenger shows that men think more about their own personal needs, including sexual needs, than women do.[76] Further, there's a wealth of research showing that women are socialised to be more concerned with the perceptions and experiences of others than men are, and to suppress their own desires. Men are thus more likely to ask for the things that make them happy and politely refuse when someone comes at them with an unwanted butt plug.

Almost all of the men I've been with seem to think it is very important that they experience pleasure and achieve orgasms. As indeed it is. Many of the women I've been with have been content to give, give, give, and watch me come with an air of satisfaction, while being frustratingly unwilling to answer the question 'what can I do for YOU?' They can come on their own, but it takes time and effort, and they don't want to ask me to, say, slowly rub their glans for twenty minutes (which, for the record, I would be only too delighted to do). They want to put out, but they don't want to put me out. It's like they think that their pleasure is secondary to their partner's. And am I innocent of this kind of behaviour? Nope.

There have certainly been times, always with men, when I've quietly curled up and acted satisfied when I was anything but. I could have told the partners in question exactly what to do to get me off, but they were done, and they wanted to go to sleep, so I decided it could wait 'til morning. And, in a scarier vein, there have been times when sex has been really quite unpleasant – too hard and fast without enough foreplay, for example – where I have just taken it rather than communicating that I wasn't enjoying what was happening. I didn't want to bruise egos. I wanted at least one of us to be having a good time. I didn't want to be shit in bed.

On reflection, my behaviour shows that I believe that my pleasure is not as important as my partner's. This is hardly surprising given representations of and attitudes to male and female sexual pleasure in media, pornography, and even medical and scientific literature. It is also hardly surprising given the tendency that I described in Chapter One of women to desire male approval, and, of course, of women to think less than men about their personal needs. All the same, I'm ashamed of myself. I'm such a strong egalitarian in the real world; why am I reverting to subservience in the bedroom?

In *The Myth of Mars and Venus,* Deborah Cameron, a professor of language and communication at Oxford, debunks a lot of commonly held beliefs about linguistic differences between men and women, pointing out that there's as much communication variation within genders as there is between genders, and arguing that what linguistic differences do exist between men and women are driven by the need to construct and project (I would say 'perform') personal meaning and identity. A common myth is that men communicate more directly than women, and thus find it difficult to understand nuanced forms of communication. Cameron explains that all people, not just women, hedge refusals in soft ways – we very rarely say 'no' outright: we offer excuses or apologies when we turn down the offers of others so as not to offend or anger them.[77]

This linguistic behaviour persists in sexual situations meaning that where two people want different things, there can be an excuse for the person who privileges their needs to pretend not to understand signals like 'I'm tired', or 'I have a headache' and to continue to perform the acts that they want. For Cameron, this is not a case of miscommunication, as it is so consistently framed in rape trials (where victims are blamed for not saying 'no' forcefully and directly, in a manner completely out of sync with how we use language). Rather, it is a case of one person privileging what they want over what another person wants.

Rape is the ugliest end of the spectrum, but even in cases

where there is consent but desires for different acts, the way that humans communicate refusal can give one partner an excuse to ignore the other's displeasure for the sake of their own. And when you have a sexual culture in which women regard their pleasure as secondary to that of their partner, this can result in the replication of acts that men desire, that have their roots in violent pornography and widespread ignorance of female sexual function.

SEX SCEPTICAL

Am I being a total buzzkill? I hope not, because I think sex in the twenty-first century is amazing. Sure, there are some weird porny elements to it, and many of us have had some less than rad experiences, but, in general, we're having an excellent time in each other's pants. There are vibrators! And bed bondage kits! And, while female orgasms might remain more elusive in our sexual culture, most partners recognise that they have clit duties to carry out from time to time. Long live the sexual revolution! It's unarguably a lot better than the repression and punishment of female sexual agency that came before.

Some women like it hardcore, some like their waxes, their corsets, their stockings, their pole-dancing classes, their *Fifty Shades*, their sexual submission, their vibrating anal beads. Why should they have to apologise for what makes them wet? Are we going to shame them, as sexually desirous women have been shamed for so long? Or are we going to celebrate a society in which women can behave in these ways in their private lives (or even in their not so private lives) without becoming immoral outcasts, unworthy of society's respect or protection?

I'm not into slut-shaming or kink-shaming. Your dog leash makes you whine – fine. And, again, as with porn, I can't claim to occupy any moral high ground here. I've participated in most of the practices listed above to a greater or lesser degree (vibrating anal beads – don't knock 'em 'til you've tried 'em). If truth be told, I have some fantasies and kinks that I probably wouldn't admit to in polite feminist company, although, interestingly, these are effortlessly and unintentionally changing as I get older and more politicised. (Perhaps because with a less gendered worldview comes broader conceptualisations of what is sexy – but we'll return to that in the next chapter.)

There is both structure and agency, and while all consent-ing adults should have the agency to exercise their desires (with other consenting adults), we also have to recognise that these desires don't materialise from thin air. While I'm not asking anyone to apologise for what gets them off, I am increasingly questioning the politics of my own sexual practices – of the sex acts I perform, how that affects the person I am, and what kind of society it both reflects and creates. It's perfectly clear that the vilification of extra-marital female sexual desire in Victorian Britain or post-independence Ireland represented the deeper misogynistic bedrock of those societies; shouldn't it also be obvious that twenty-first-century sexual culture reflects the gender politics of our times?

In the book *Female Chauvinist Pigs*, Ariel Levy describes

how issues of sex positivity, sexual liberation, pornography and choice split the feminist movement in the seventies and eighties.[78] (I'll give a summary here, but Levy's account is really great. I also recommend Bell Hook's chapter on sexuality in *Feminism is for Everybody*, which provides crucial insights into the lesbian aspects of the sex positivity debate.[79])

In the early stages of second-wave feminism, the women's movement and the sexual revolution were lovingly intertwined, sharing a mistrust of conventional family arrangements and repressive laws regarding sexuality and reproductive rights. The legalisation of the birth control pill and the decriminalisation of abortion were successes for both movements. Hugh Heffner even contributed funding to the legal battle for both of these monumental advances. As Levy puts it: 'the larger reimagining of sexual pleasure as a crucial part of life – one worth fighting for and talking about – and the sense that sexual freedom was ultimately *political*, were shared tenets of both the women's movement and the sexual revolution.'

However, the kind of sexual freedom being fought for by Heffner and his ilk was different to the kind being fought for by feminists. Asked if he'd like his daughter, then fourteen, to appear in *Playboy* one day, Heffner said he would see it as a compliment to his work, but that he would not like her to be promiscuous or immoral. As Levy observes, in Heffner's sexual revolution, female sexuality could only be performance: 'a show of sexiness, not an indication of an unbridled sexuality like his own.' Meanwhile, in the new sexually permissive climate, hardcore pornography flourished, causing feminist ire at increasingly acceptable depictions of sexual violence against women.

In the late seventies a group of prominent members of the women's movement began to focus their energies on fighting pornography. Robin Morgan coined the slogan 'Pornography is the theory, rape is the practice.' Susan Brownmiller's 1975 publication *Against Our Will: Men, Women and Rape* situated rape as 'nothing more or less than a conscious process of intimidation by which *all men* keep *all women* in a state of fear,' and called porn 'the undiluted essence of anti-female propaganda'. In Minneapolis in 1983, Catherine McKinnon and Andrea Dworkin even teamed up with conservative politicians – politicians opposed to abortion and to gay rights – to try to ban pornography in the city.

According to Levy, the pornography wars of the seventies and eighties caused an unbridged and unbridgeable schism in the second-wave women's movement. Against the anti-porn feminists 'were the women who felt that if feminism was about freedom for women, then women should be free to look at or appear in pornography.' These women characterised themselves as sex-positive. They'd fought for sexual freedom, and they weren't going to be told what to do in the bedroom by the priest, the pastor, Morgan, Brownmiller, Dworkin, or anyone. As Bell Hooks points out, lesbians engaged in S&M relationships and sexual practices were often doubly criticised by their anti-porn feminist sisters, adding a layer of homophobia to what was already seen by many as an assault on the hard-won sexual agency of women. This tension in the feminist movement has never been resolved. To this day, some feminists regard sex (or even sex work) as liberation, and others as subjugation.

Like so many feminists, I feel torn between the recognition that something is rotten in our sexual state, and the awareness that I am simply a product of this culture, with all the attendant kinks and fantasies, and if there's one time I don't have to think about equality, surely it's with a beautiful body in a big bouncy bed. Can't I be a feminist and still like it when lovers tie me up and do unspeakable things to me?

I used to think that the answer to this question was: yes, undoubtedly. But, increasingly, I'm not so sure. It is so clear to me that binary understandings of sex (male/female; top/bottom; dominant/submissive, etc.) are related to unequal power relations in society. And when people try to argue that what happens in bedrooms can be siphoned off from social reality – that sex based on dominance is neither a product of nor producer of patriarchy – I rarely find their arguments well-reasoned or convincing. I want to. Oh how I want to. But I just don't. Sex is a powerful, gendered part of the social world, and, as such, it powerfully affects the ways in which we perform our gender roles.

A BDSM 'Master' near Palm Springs, California, hosts a two-week summer retreat yearly to 'provide a safe and welcoming, private place (and opportunity) for White Masters and plantation slaves/n*ggers to meet and explore their mutual fantasies.' The summer sex camp is for consenting male adults, all of whom are exercising their sexual agency. Here's an extract from an explanatory posting by the host, 'Massa Warren' (Master Warren) on the 'Slave Ownership Southern Style' Yahoo group:

The minimum requirement for slaves is that they be obedient and respectful of all Masters and work to give the Masters an enjoyable time. This can be anything from preparing and serving drinks and meals, doing housework or yard work, to providing sexual relief on demand, to hard labor in the compound (depending on the slave's previously-stated limitations). Slaves should expect Masters to be totally comfortable and free in using humiliating or degrading racist speech in referring to or speaking to mud-slaves. It's not all punishment and misery for slaves... there is plenty of time for cama-raderie and playful fun also. Some slaves even form a brotherly bond with the other slaves that serve with them. Masters also form lasting bonds and friendships based on their mutual interests and sharing slaves.

It's just a small friendly gathering of White Masters at my house/compound... being served by mud-slaves as might have been in a modern version of slave-days. One might call it a situation of consensual non-consent/ slavery. Slaves can set their limits and the time they will be in service as slaves in advance... and also what they expect to learn and experience from the experience. The more that a slave lets me know about itself in advance, the better I can guide its growth from the experience.

No one is forcing anyone to partake in this sexual game. I have no doubt that many of the black subs experience sexual pleasure from their domination by these white doms. I also know that there exist some sub/dom gay relationships in which black men dom white men. (I don't have the research to back this up, but I would imagine, that, just like female dom/male sub relationships they are the exception rather than the rule – perhaps so much so that white subs pay black doms, just as many male subs pay for female domination.)

Having spent time reading through the posts on the Slave Ownership Southern Style Yahoo group (an experience I would not wish on any other human being), it would be very difficult to convince me that this race-based role play bears no relation to racism in society. It uses the language and symbolism of white supremacy, and even refers to the biological predisposition of the subs to servitude (quote: 'This is intended for genetically-bred plantation-n*gger slaveboys, mainly because they have so few places to comfortably explore their natural slave nature in the presence of true White Masters').*

It would be equally difficult to convince me that the white men who organise this event are not racist. And I saw evidence that at least some of the black men participating are torn between their sexual desires and the knowledge that their sexual desires are the result of some pretty fucked up shit. I don't believe that the men partaking in this event can possibly go back out into the world without a weakened or destroyed sense of racial equality. And I am angered by the suggestion that there is any biological, 'natural' basis for this fetishisation of white power and black servitude: it is clearly related to history and to culture.

The racism here is so easy to see. But we have a gendered

---

* I first came across this story on Chauncey Devega's fascinating blog *We Are Respectable Negroes*. See Devega, Chauncey, 'Playing with Sex, Power, and Race: Did You Know That There Are "Plantation Retreats" Where Black People Go to Serve Their White "Masters?"', *We Are Respectable Negroes*, 12 Aug 2012.

sexual culture in which female submission is normal – where most doms are men and most subs are women, where *Fifty Shades of Grey* sells 100 million copies, where porn is all about women choking on cocks and rubbing come out of their eyes – yet we can't recognise the sexism.

Titles like Jenna Jameson's *How to Make Love Like a Porn Star* fly off the shelves, while the internal clitoris is absent from anatomy textbooks. The porn aesthetic is now so mainstream that it's in everything from Pot Noodle adverts to music videos aimed at teens, yet women feel uncomfortable publically breast feeding. At Trinity College Dublin, where I did my Master's degree, you can now join a Pole Dancing Society, while women in Dublin cannot access safe, legal abortion. Corporations take male clients to clubs where women are paid cash to writhe naked in their laps, and then expect these same clients to respect their female employees? Young women are conditioned to costume themselves in an aesthetic congruent with the sex and porn industry, yet are blamed for doing so if they get raped. Women hate their bodies and value their partner's sexual pleasure over their own, yet claim to be sexually liberated. We are ostensibly free to have sex with whom-ever we like (if we don't care about being sluts rather than studs), yet we perform this liberation in costumes and choreography that, at best, symbolise shame of our adult physicalities, or, at worst, degrade and hurt us.

In these contradictions, don't we have as perfect a mirror of our society's gender politics as compulsory female extra-marital chastity gave us of gender politics in the past? In them, there's a crystalline reflection of a society in which women are legally equal, but materially unequal. There's a synecdoche of a world in which our inequality is ever and always explained as a product of our choices, of our agency, instead of in terms of the structures that created us, and within which we continue to act.

There is something very wrong with our sexual performances. Does this statement make me sex negative? All I know is that I love sex, but I can't keep ignoring the parallels between the way I practise it and the way gender inequality operates in the society around me.

I can imagine a world in which we stop ascribing power primarily to individuals in masculine bodies, cease to attach greater importance to the sexual pleasure of men, and start to recognise that each human is a unique sexual being – both physically and psychologically – with whom the act of sex must be joyously discovered and negotiated anew. Do I think that this means we'll all put away our whips and paddles, our buzzy toys, our sense of transgressive, anarchic, inhibitionless fun? No: in fact, I think that in a sexual era based on equality, where we don't start by playing limiting roles in the first place, the games we'll play will proliferate in endless kinkalicious variety.

STAGE A SEX SCENE

Get a group of friends together to talk about sex. Not like Carrie and company, and dropping the 'I'm a naughty, strawberry-flavoured, frilly Cosmo sex goddess' act that we've all been told is our appropriate, liberated, twenty-first-century woman demeanour. Get a group of friends together to talk honestly about sex. I believe in women-only[*] spaces when it comes to these kinds of discussions.

Make a list of things you want to discuss. Pornography, for example, and how it has impacted on your sexual experiences. How your pleasure functions versus how partners – particularly male partners – have expected it to function. Or maybe the power relations present in your sex life and how you reconcile them with your feminism. Maybe sexual violence or coercion you've experienced. Regards the last one, I have been shocked (and deeply affected) at how many of my strong female friends have had traumatic sexual encounters that they don't speak about, of which they feel ashamed and even guilty.

Get used to articulating your experiences, desires, and worries surrounding sex in a safe and supportive space, and help each other to come up with strategies for speaking in the heat of the moment when it is more difficult to do so.

Performing new sexual roles in real life can be intimidating, especially if you're not sure what to ask for. Something that has helped me is writing my own erotica. I definitely recommend giving it a go – it's fun, it's hot, it's challenging, and it really makes you think about the origins of your desires. So create some smoking scenes that emphasise female experience, and that weave the reality of your body and the complexities of your politics into the scenarios that turn you on. Next thing you know, you'll be turning fiction into fact.

---

[*] 'Women-only spaces' in my feminist politics always include gender-queer people and trans-women. They also welcome trans-men who feel as though the space is relevant to their gendered experiences.

CHAPTER TEN:
ROLE PLAY

'Under the authority of a language that had been care-
fully expurgated so that it was no longer directly named,
sex was taken charge of, tracked down as it were, by a
discourse that aimed to allow it no obscurity, no respite.'

Michel Foucault[80]

MAKING AN ENTRANCE (COMING OUT?)

I've had romantic and sexual relationships with women as
well as men since my teens. I don't consider myself bisexual.
I don't really believe in bisexual. First, there are not two
different kinds of people to whom I'm attracted. There are
infinite kinds of people to whom I'm attracted: I've fancied
beardy, strong-armed, imposing men in army boots and shy,
fey boys in skinny tank tops; I've fancied curvy, be-spectacled
nerd girls and tall, elegant femmes in perfect eyeliner.*

---

* Some gender and sexuality activists feel comfortable with and proud of the
term bisexual, which is a stance I respect greatly. Check out Julia Serrano's book,
Excluded, for an excellent defence of the term and interesting argument (which
I don't fully agree with) as to why more queer-identified people should embrace
it. See: Serrano, Julia. *Excluded: Making Feminist and Queer Movements More*
Inclusive. Berkeley: Seal Press, (2013): pp. 81–99.

Don't I have a preference? Okay, if I'm utterly honest, there's one thing that consistently turns my head: boyish girls or girlish boys. But androgyny wasn't always my thing. When I loved the beard-man, I used to find other beards attractive. And even now that I consistently find myself creepily following androgynes around parties, a quick chat can leave me cold for them, and hot for their unequivocally masculine or feminine friend.

Second, I don't have two different kinds of sex. I have infinite kinds of sex, and it seems to bear really very little relation to the kind of genitalia my lovers have. My experience has been that women tend to be both more sexually generous than men and less willing to accept generosity, but outside of that (clearly socially conditioned) phenomenon, I've had sex with men that's been queerer than folk, and sex with women that feels conservatively hetero. I've played dominant with dudes; I've played submissive with ladies. And my most profound and fulfilling sexual relationships have been based on love, equality and intimacy, not biological sex, gender or sexuality. Trust makes me freaky!

Some people might call me pansexual or sapiosexual, but the word I like for my sexuality is 'queer'. Where 'bisexual' buoys up the boundaries between male and female, gay and straight, that I have long ceased to believe in, 'queer' lets me exist on a spectrum. It's more fun outside the box.

When people notice that I date both men and women, they often ask me when I knew that I liked girls too. The most honest answer would probably be 'when I had my tongue in one's mouth', but that doesn't seem to cut it. It feels like, for people to accept my queerness, I'm supposed to have experienced deep sexual desire for women from a young age, have tried – experiencing much psychological distress – to fight it, and have failed. It feels like I'm supposed to have had irresistible, guilty, erotic fantasies about my school friends or female pop stars from the time I first became aware of my clitoris, or somehow my sexuality doesn't count.

I could always tell that other women were attractive. I liked looking at women in swimsuits as much as I liked looking at men in swimsuits. But I think most of my female friends could tell that other women were attractive too. We had excellent training in this aesthetic task from the media. I also think most of my male friends could tell that other men were attractive.

When I was about ten, a twelve-year-old boy I was close to asked me in a worried tone: 'you can tell when girls are good-looking, can't you?' I could and I said so. 'Yeah, and boys can tell when other boys are good-looking too – that's just normal, isn't it?' In my ten-year-old wisdom I thought it probably was. 'It doesn't mean you're gay,' he concluded, clearly unconvinced. I offered some reassurance. (He's pretty much the straightest adult you're ever going to meet, in case you were wondering.)

When I was fifteen I told my four best girlfriends that I wanted to try sleeping with a women sometime – just to see what it was like. Three of them said that they would too. Weren't we quite the progressive bunch of Irish lasses? In short, in my early teens, I don't think I was a whole lot gayer or straighter than anybody else.

When I was eighteen, I shared a bed with an older woman

after a party (she was in her mid-twenties – ancient!) and made out with her. In the morning we laughed about it, and I didn't give it much further thought.

When I was nineteen, I met Máire through mutual friends. She was super smart, super cool, super pretty and super lesbian. I flirted my ass off with her, and heard through the grapevine that she liked me. I sent word through the grapevine that I liked her back. Then one night we ended up alone, in a hot tub, kissing less and less gently. I remember thinking at first 'oh my God, I'm with a girl! For real! What does this mean about who I am?!' But then I got distracted. In the morning our friends had pinned a sign that said 'Jacuzzi Floozies' to the door of our room, and henceforth were we known.

Until I was intimate with Máire, I didn't know whether or not I was going to be turned on by, or be able to have an orgasm with, another woman. What I'm trying to say is that my sexual desire for her didn't stem from some deep, irrepressible internal identity, but from curiosity, adventurousness and a thirst for new things. For some reason, however, this seemed to piss everyone off.

An ex called my new romance 'tacky'. A friend accused me of attention seeking and trying to impress boys (amazing how even having sex with another woman has to be read in terms of male pleasure). I've lost count of the number of people who've told me that while they are okay with gay, they're not okay with bi. One friend said that if I liked both men and women, why didn't I just date men? Gay friends told me to come out of the closet. Straight friends told me it was probably just a phase.

I didn't know. Maybe it *was* just a phase. Probably I'd get a boyfriend in the end and marry him and be 'normal', but in the meantime I wasn't going to worry too much about it – coming out was for gay people, I had boyfriends more often than girlfriends anyway, and it just didn't seem like a particularly massive deal.

Over a decade later, I no longer have any strong desire for a monogamous male life partner, and it seems that my sexuality really is one of the primary things that people use to define me. Just ignoring my queerness is no longer an option.

Based on his study of the sexual habits of hundreds of men in the late forties, Alfred Kinsey famously said that there's no such thing as 'straight' or 'gay', simply a propensity to engage in homosexual or heterosexual acts. The Kinsey scale goes from zero to six, where zero means experience of and desire for only hetero acts, and six means experience of and desire for only homo acts. There's also an X category for people with no sexual desire or experience. Everything else falls along a spectrum. His later research with women supported this conclusion too.

This makes intuitive sense to me. If I chose to, I could almost certainly act straight, and the more my sexual relationships fell under that umbrella, the more my sexual memories and desires would be hetero. Equally, if I chose to, I could almost certainly act lesbian, and the more my relationships and sexual practices fell within that realm, the gayer I'd be. But this is just me: as the Kinsey Scale suggests, different people experience their orientations differently.

Modern science suggests that orientations are likely to be

partly based in genetics. However, this doesn't mean that some people have a 'gay gene' that makes them homosexual. Rather, as genetics professor Jenny Graves explains, even the inherited basis of sexual orientation is a spectrum rather than a binary. According to Graves:

> It's a bit like height, which is influenced by variants in thousands of genes, as well as the environment, and produces a 'continuous distribution' of people of different heights. At the two extremes are the very tall and the very short.
>
> In the same way, at each end of a continuous distribution of human mating preference, we would expect the 'very male-loving' and the 'very female-loving' in both sexes.[81]

My desire has been largely conditioned, of course, by society (structure). One of the things I like about being with men is that it's so easy – both sexually and socially. Everyone knows how things are supposed to go: it's been drilled into us from the earliest point. Hetero can be lazy, and lazy can be nice. Perhaps paradoxically then, one of the things I like about being with women is that I don't have a blueprint – I feel like the script is written afresh every time. It's exciting, and sometimes confusing, and it definitely creates an intimacy that can be lacking from hetero flings. My sexuality is also in part a choice (agency). And perhaps one of the things that highlights this most clearly for me is that when someone is unlikely to return my desire, I'm really great at shutting attraction down. So I meet a beautiful man, but he's gay: I stop wanting to sleep with him. I meet a beautiful woman, but she's straight: I stop wanting to sleep with her. I meet a beautiful person but they're in a monogamous relationship: I stop wanting to sleep with them. My experience of sexual desire is not one of base biology, but of allowing feelings and relationships to develop where it's clear to me that everyone in the situation is excited for this to happen.

When people tell me that these ways of thinking about sexuality are 'unnatural' (the worst argument against anything ever, in my opinion), I sometimes ask them to think about their relationships with their first cousins. Most will say that they never have sexual thoughts about their cousins. I know I haven't (sorry, cousin darlings, ye're all totally gorgeous, but I've been socially conditioned and all). But just a few generations ago in Western society, cousin marriage was perfectly normal and we know that lots of people did have sexual desire for their cousins.

Our desire is partially based on the people we're told we're allowed to desire. I have a 'not for sexytime' box into which I put hot straight girls, gay boys, people who've made it clear that they're not interested, people in monogamous relationships, friends and relatives. I do all this subconsciously, but it's also clear, from looking at my crushes and relationships, that I definitely do it.

When I talk about what is for me the evident fact that our sexual identities are, in large part, products of our society and our choices, lots of people say – 'that's not true. I have absolutely no [same-sex/opposite-sex] desire whatsoever! It must be biological, because I'm fine with [gay people/straight people], but the thought of touching someone's [vagina/penis] makes me feel sick!' Yeah, well the thought of shagging one of my cousins makes me feel sick, but I can still logically admit that this is a learned aversion.

When people say they have no same-sex desire I believe them, absolutely. But I equally believe that in a different society, this wouldn't be the case. If they were pre-marriage-age men in Ancient Greece, for example, they would be expected to experience romantic and sexual desire for teenage boys. This attraction was supposed to be based on admiration for the boy's beauty and virtue and, in a society of arranged opposite-sex marriage, it was the only relationship in most Hellenic men's lives in which they would have to court their beloved.

When the boy (who, as a male citizen of Greece, was of the most important demographic of the time) had accepted the older gent's advances, he was taken under a manly wing, brought to political and social events and, of course, initiated sexually. This was a completely normal and socially sanctioned stage of male life in Ancient Greece – it would have been considered weird for men *not* to find teenage boys romantically and sexually attractive.

Today, thankfully, most Western men say they do not desire to woo and sleep with fifteen-year-old boys. But they should be able to admit that if they were born in Ancient Greece, this would be different.

I have a queer friend who is almost exclusively attracted to 'bois' or to biologically female queers (sometimes transgender) who look, dress and to some extent act like young men. I have another friend who is almost exclusively attracted to people, either male or female, with tattoo'd arm sleeves, plug-stretched ear lobes and copious metal hanging from their septums and lips. These categories of people did not even exist thirty years ago.

Sexuality then, is about individual preference, but it's also about socially constructed categories of people. Sexuality is a kind of role play. And if we live in a society where we are divided up into men and women, gay and straight, then of course this dictates the kinds of sexualities we develop and the kinds of romantic relationships we form.

I can have no idea what my sexuality would look like if I'd been brought up in a society that taught children that same-sex desire is normal and healthy, and that sexuality is both a spectrum and something that changes throughout one's lifetime. I was trying to imagine it with my friend Jim one night – he thinks I'm repressed and, in such a society, I'd probably be lesbian. I was talking about it with my friend Becky another night – she thinks I'm trying to prove some kind of feminist point by sleeping with women, so she reckons I'd probably be straight. Sigh. Why are we so obsessed with these pigeonholes?

I'LL PLAY THE HETERO, YOU PLAY THE HOMO

Many of us strongly believe that people are either gay or straight (or maybe one of those pesky bisexuals). We think that desiring and/or performing sex acts with people of the opposite or same sex constitutes a part of our innermost identities.

In his influential 1976 book *The History of Sexuality*, the philosopher Michel Foucault challenges the ideology of the sexual revolution. According to the wisdom of his times (and ours, I would argue), sexuality is viewed as a 'natural' part of human identity, which was repressed in Western culture from the seventeenth century onwards. Then along came psychoanalysis, revealing our 'true' sexual natures, followed by the sexual revolution, allowing us happy, healthy, open sexual identities.[82]

For Foucault this is the wrong way round. Modern society has not unearthed the truth about human sexuality – it has simply created new categories into which people are grouped. He points out that talking about sex and desire has long existed in the Catholic practice of confession. In the late nineteenth century, this practice morphed into psychoanalysis: subjects were now encouraged to confess their deepest, darkest desires to the scientific priest, who gave them newly constructed identity categories – homo or hetero – through which to understand their thoughts and actions.

In the eighteenth, nineteenth, and early twentieth centuries, sex started to be seen as the bedrock of our personalities and identities. For Foucault, this social trend allowed the dominant class in the new democratic, capitalist era – the bourgeoisie – to taxonomise and control people. If we can pigeonhole individuals and authoritatively say that they have certain kinds of histories, psychologies and capabilities because of the sexual acts that they desire and perform, then we can control society's attitudes towards them, and control their behaviour too. For Foucault, power is not top down – something implemented by the state or the dominant classes – but rather it exists in the relations between people and institutions. It is because we ourselves believe that our historically constructed sexualities are crucial parts of our identities that we can be convinced to organise our emotions, relationships and families in ways most beneficial to a capitalist society.

Jonathan Katz, in his book *The Invention of Heterosexuality*, puts the historical construction of sexuality as identity under the spotlight in an eye-opening way. He points out that the term homosexual was only invented in 1868, and the term heterosexual dates, arguably, to 1892. He says: 'before that, if words are clues to concepts, people did not conceive of a social universe polarised into heteros and homos.'[83]

Katz is sceptical of people who try to project 'hetero' and 'homo' identities onto opposite- or same-sex love in past societies, reminding us that past societies organised people and sexuality along very different lines. For example, in Ancient Greece, romantic love was thought to exist primarily between people of the same sex. Katz calls into question the 'common sense' contemporary assumption that while the word 'heterosexual' might not have existed prior to 1892, the feelings and acts we associate with it did.

Katz rips apart three arguments for the existence of an age-old heterosexuality: 1) That as humans must procreate or perish, heterosexuality is an everlasting necessity; 2) That as all societies recognise basic distinctions between male and female, biological and cultural difference implies historical heterosexuality; 3) That the ways in which men and women experience bodily pleasure is the basis of an unchanging heterosexuality.

Katz convincingly argues that we don't need heterosexuality in order for reproductive sex to exist, nor for distinctions between male and female to exist, nor for the existence of sexual pleasure between men and women. Katz says: heterosexuality 'signifies one particular historical arrangement of the sexes and their pleasures [...] Sexual reproduction, sexual difference and sexual pleasure have been combined in different cultures in radically different ways.'[84]

Katz asks us to think about why we talk about transvestitism – the desire to dress in the clothes of the opposite sex – while we do not talk about the equally mysterious desire to dress in the clothes of one's own sex. With transsexualism, we talk about the desire to inhabit the body of the other sex, but we don't talk about the feeling of being the same sex. For Katz, the 'desire to maintain the integrity of our sex' is something to be explained every bit as much as transexualism.

Equally, by putting 'heterosexuality' under the spotlight as itself a recent invention, Katz shakes up the idea that there are biologically- or socially-normal sexual behaviours associated with existing in a male body or a female body. In fact, he calls the idea that hetero and homo feelings are legitimated through biological or social determinants 'a widely held late-twentieth-century US folk belief'. He even goes so far as to compare the idea of universal male–female pleasure sex to the Victorian belief that masturbation causes blindness. And just think of all the lovely times Victorian ladies could have had on their own in the dark if they'd only seen through the ruse.

FANTASIES

The idea of immutable sexual and gender identities has been crucial to the movements for women's rights and for LGBTQ rights. Feminist theorist Joan Scott writes about the importance of studying the essentialist fantasies that formed necessary parts of certain feminist movements – for instance, the fantasy of woman as mother, or the fantasy of woman as orator (by which Scott means women who take on traditionally male roles in the public sphere). These fantasies gloss over the differences between women, making a seemingly coherent category that can help activists to achieve social change in particular situations.[85]

If I create a fantasy of woman as orator, I can argue for the rights of all women to work alongside men in professional realms, by saying that this is woman's nature. Similarly, patriarchal fantasies – of woman as gentle and domestic, for example – make a coherent category that maintains an oppressive order. So there's a lot of power in fantasy, and concentrating on the fantasies needed by different groups at certain points of history allows us to talk about that time and place without falling into the trap of essentialising – without having to say 'woman, by her nature, is…'

We use fantasy similarly when talking about sexuality

today. Essentialist categories of gay and straight have never been more concrete in popular culture. This glossing over of difference has a function, of course, just as feminist fantasies had in the past. It allows rights groups to say: 'this is our immutable, unchanging and unchangeable identity. We are what we are. We deserve rights.' It allows LGBTQ marchers to shout: 'we're here, we're queer, get used to it!'

The essential fantasy of the person born gay with no opposite sex attraction supports an identity politics that works against homophobic groups who want to construct gayness as a sinful lifestyle choice, which the gay person could 'correct' if s/he wanted. So the gay fantasy is a powerful and necessary one, but a fantasy all the same. And if we want to forge a society that is not based on male/female binaries, then we need to move beyond it.

I realise that this argument is uncomfortable when identity politics are still being used to achieve concrete political aims in our homophobic society. But in order to achieve both gender and LGBTQ equality, we need to unsettle the now institutionalised binary categories of homosexual and heterosexual in the same way that heterosexuality was destabilised by the gay rights movement of the sixties, seventies and eighties. We need to stop saying 'LGBTQ is', 'Man is', or 'Woman is' and to think of both gender and sexuality as spectrums. The fantasies, once liberating, ultimately sustain divisions between gay people and straight people, between women and men.

SEX BEYOND THE ACT

When we eliminate the social stigma attached to acting outside of gender roles, I suspect that the people we are attracted to will change. Why do I think this?

Lovers were able to learn to associate my hairy legs – a masculine physical characteristic, which they wouldn't normally find attractive – with me: a person they liked and were attracted to. I have a straight guy friend who fell in love with a trans woman, and learned to associate her penis – a male physical characteristic which he wouldn't usually find attractive – with his girlfriend: a person he was attracted to.

The gay artist Bill Roundy has a lovely, clever comic strip called 'Orientation Police', which you can find online, about falling in love with a trans man, and learning to associate his vagina – a female physical characteristic which he wouldn't usually find attractive – with his boyfriend: a person he was attracted to.

Queer theorist Jack/Judith Halberstam believes that we're entering a post-transsexual era. In the same way that homosexuality was invented at the end of the nineteenth century, he believes that the 'sexual body', or the idea that a body can be made to 'match' our gender identities, was invented at the end of the twentieth century. He thinks that we are now experiencing a boundary change, but this doesn't mean that we'll all start to surgically alter our sex; rather, it means that we will begin to acknowledge the ways in which we have already altered ourselves. For Halberstam, we're all transsexuals. He says:

> We are all cross-dressers but where are we crossing from and to what? There is no 'other' side, no 'opposite' sex, no natural divide to be spanned by surgery, by disguise, by passing. We all pass or we don't, we all wear our drag, and we all derive a different degree of pleasure – sexual or otherwise – from our costumes. It is just that for some of us, our costumes are made of fabric or material, while for others they are made of skin; for some an outfit can be changed; for others skin must be resown.[86]

These might seem like radical ideas – that there is, fundamentally, no universal biological or social imperative for heterosexual behaviour, and that our sexual identities do not follow logically from biological sex, but are, rather, a complex interplay of sex, orientation and gender identity.

The ideas seem radical, because they're at odds with our experiences of ourselves. The statement 'I am straight and I love my boyfriend' feels true to many women, and indeed it is true. As Katz remarks, to examine the history and present of 'sexed feelings, sexed bodies and sexed clothes', is not to criticise anyone's heterosexuality. It's not an attack on heterosexual feeling or identity to point out that it is culturally and historically specific, rather than eternal or universal.

To return to the ideas of Judith Butler that we looked at in Chapter Five, gender identity is performative, which means that it's not some unchanging core of 'me-ness' or 'you-ness', but something that we perform into being through acts over time. Sexual identity, often related to gender identity, is similar. This was highlighted for me recently when talking to polyamorous friends,* who consider the non-monogamous ways they've structured their romantic lives as part of their sexual identities. Polyamory isn't just something they do; it's something they are. (I'm not going to talk more about polyamory or alternative romantic relationships here, but it'll probably be the subject of my next book.)

Sleeping with men, women, both or neither isn't simply something one does, but something one is. But it's important to remember that the 'is' here comes to be through perform-ance – through acts repeated over time. And these acts are socially influenced. When we recognise this, then it's not much of a leap to suggest that in a society that isn't based on gender binaries we'll be less attracted to the kind of genitalia people have, and more attracted to an infinitely more exciting blend of the physical and psychological.

---

* Polyamory, or ethical non-monogamy, is the practice of having more than one intimate partner at a time, with the knowledge and consent of everyone involved.

CHAPTER ELEVEN:
KNOW THY AUDIENCE

'...as a strategy of survival within compulsory systems, gender is a performance with clearly punitive consequences. Discrete genders are part of what "humanizes" individuals within contemporary culture; indeed, we regularly punish those who fail to do their gender right.'

Judith Butler[87]

RED ROSES AND RAPTUROUS APPLAUSE

I'm fifteen, and Grandad O'Toole has died. As per the Irish way of things, his body is laid out in the dining room, and the good people of Galway will be dropping by all day to pay their respects. My grandad was well-known, had nine children, and upwards of twenty-five grandchildren. The stream of locals offering their condolences is thick and steady; it's hard to wriggle through the hall. It is imperative that every drop in the stream be drinking a cup of tea or glass of whiskey and eating a ham sandwich or this would be a very atypical occasion altogether. Granny must be there to greet them all and accept the sympathies. This lovely

Irish way of marking death looks seamless to many of those passing through; it flows effortlessly from history, culture and community – a current of life in which we all know how to sail.

But below deck, of course, there's a tight crew of women keeping everything afloat. My little cousin Róisín dives unnoticed through the tall, tightly-packed visitors, gathering up china to bring to the kitchen. I have my hands sudsey in the sink, and am passing clean delft to my mum, who's drying it and placing it on a tray for re-distribution. My aunties Anne and Marcella have formed a sandwich production line of staggering industry – slapping pan with butter and ham, slicing the soft, layered squares into triangles, and arranging everything neatly on platters.

Auntie Maria is overseeing the continual boiling of the kettle, the circulation of pots of fresh tea, and milk jug and sugar bowl levels. Occasionally a male head pops in: 'Would we have a glass of water for Mrs Lyons? She needs to take her tablet.' We are chattering, us women in the engine room, and I'm content to be helping. Although it doesn't cross my mind, it would feel weird and wrong to be sitting in the next room with my brothers and male relatives when Mum and the other women are working so hard to keep everything flowing.

Enter my cousin Sarah from next door, where she's been sitting beside the fire with the boys, eating currant cake and drinking tea. Bell Hooks says that feminists are made, not born, but she hadn't met Sarah O'Toole. At the time Grandad dies, Sarah is nineteen, and she has exactly zero interest in being the domestic, subservient little girl that the world would like her to be. I don't think she'll mind me saying that this didn't exactly make her the family's golden child.

She walks in and says 'look at all the women in the kitchen, while the men sit next door doing nothing.' The aunties ignore her. 'Emer, why don't you ask Ronan or Ciarán to take over for a bit? You don't have to do everything just because you're a girl.' I'd always looked up to brainy, talented Sarah – she played in grunge bands and had hot, long-haired boyfriends and taught herself how to speak Russian from tapes – so it hurts when I think she's having a dig.

'I'm not helping because I'm a girl,' I say emphatically, 'I'm helping because my grandfather just died. I'm not in charge of nagging Ronan and Ciarán – I mean, they should be helping, but it's not my fault if they're being lazy. I'm helping because I want to make things easier for Granny and everyone else. What the boys do is their own business. I'm *not* helping just because I'm a girl.'

'Well said, Emer,' sang the aunties, 'that's right!' Mum was punch proud. Sarah retreated, defeated, to the sitting room. The status quo had been defended by the rhetoric of agency and choice and now we could all go back to performing our socially sanctioned gender roles, safe in the knowledge that the silly lazy feminist (who really just didn't want to get off her arse and help like a good girl) had been put so artfully in her place.

News of my heroic speech spread like wildfire. 'And then Emer said to her...' I heard an auntie's voice pass to an uncle. 'Fair play!' they exclaimed, smiling, delighted, 'isn't she a mighty woman?'

I continued my selfless helper act for the rest of the funeral. When my little cousins were misbehaving in mass, I tapped their teary-eyed mother on the shoulder and offered to take them to a nearby playground 'til the service was over. I helped load the wreaths onto the hearse. I helped clean Granny's house before we all travelled to the burial. 'You've played a blinder,' said my uncle Mick, kindly gifting me twenty pounds. I had – I'd played a blinder! Willfully blind, I played my gender role. Everyone loved me! I had shown them how much I loved them! They threw red roses! There was a standing ovation! I was the star of the show!

ROTTEN TOMATOES AND WALK OUTS

I'm twenty-eight. I live in London, but am home for a friend's wedding. The day after the nuptials, there are casual drinks in Galway City with the bride and groom, and my brothers and I are in having the craic. Mum wants us to come out to Oranmore village, where I'm from, for dinner. I don't really want to leave the party, but I'm not back that often, and it's important to make time for the Mammy.

So we roll on home, bringing my cousin Saoirse and a college buddy of Ronan's with us. My dad is in Galway at the time, so Mum has invited him too (my parents aren't together, but they're good friends). Mum is cooking an elaborate roast dinner. When we get in the door, she hands me a pack of prawns and asks me to do something with them for a starter. I make a chilli and garlic paste, fry them up, and arrange them on beds of rocket. Mum doesn't have any: she's still cooking. As she serves her seven guests, she tells us that she has to go to choir practice, so she won't be staying to eat with us. She takes a tiny, half-plate of food for herself, sits at the very corner of the table without a placemat or anything, finishes quickly, then gets up to leave.

I'm thinking, 'this is highly weird. Isn't this highly weird? I mean, yes, Mum always waits on people, and that's weird in the typical patriarchal way that everyone just ignores, but she doesn't usually leave afterwards. This is a whole new level of weird. Isn't this a whole new level of weird?' But nobody else thinks so because they are used to women waiting on men like servants. I was used to it once too, but I've lived in London for four years and now it seems like something from an alien planet in the fifties.

Also, I'm experiencing some daughterly aggravation (which probably isn't terribly fair to Mum, who hasn't lived in London for the last four years): I didn't come to dinner in order to be waited on and fed. I came to spend time with my funny, cool mother. I'm perfectly capable of paying for a meal in a restaurant if I need service and sustenance. The thought of Mum cooking for hours for others and then not even sitting down to enjoy the meal or the company makes me really uncomfortable.

Mum grabs her bag and coat, and, as she's going out the door she says: 'Now Emer, there's some ground coffee in the press above the kettle, there's a carrot cake on the dining-room table, and there's whipped cream in the fridge. So you'll take care of that.' And off she pops.

I am not filled with feminist joy, obviously.

We finish our meal. Saoirse starts to gather the plates into a pile. The four men at the table do nothing except deign to pass her dirty crockery. I want to serve the crowd dessert and coffee about as much as I want to frenchie Nick Griffin. But, I'm a grown woman who has headed up an academic journal, organised numerous conferences, university seminars and theatre productions, and who is generally skilled at making reasonable people understand their duties to others in a group; I figure there's a way to handle things so that everyone can see what's fair and what isn't.

'I'm going to go get the dessert like Mum asked. Ronan and Ciarán, will ye clear up?'

A second where no one moves. Ronan looks at me, annoyed. Saoirse starts to clear the table. My brothers, sighing and shuffling, rise from their seats, and it looks like they're going to help. I pop the kettle on, and go next door to find cake and plates. This takes me – at the very, very most – ninety seconds.

I come back in and the four men – Ronan, Ciarán, Ronan's friend and my dad – are sitting comfortably back at the table, chatting, while Saoirse has her hands in the sink. I can't believe it.

'Lads,' I say angrily, 'what is going on? Why aren't ye clearing up?'

'It's done,' says Ronan, clearly pissed off to be nagged by his sister in front of a dude-bro. They were talking about football!

'If it's done, then why are the two women in the room

still on their feet, working, while the four men are sitting at the table? And also, it is clearly *not* done. Saoirse, sit down: you're a guest.'

Saoirse sits.

'Why do we have to do it right now? We're having a conversation,' says Ronan.

'Because ye're heading back into town soon, so if you don't do it now, it'll be left for Mum when she gets home.'

Ronan looks apologetically at his macho mate. Ciarán has his head down; he hates it when his sister goes off like this. Why is she so aggressive? The boys stay seated – they're not going to be bossed about. And then my dad starts:

'But sure cleaning up is women's work. Women are better at that kind of thing, hah? That's what women do – they wait on men. Men don't do housework. That's the way it should be. Amen't I right?'

If you were going to be kind about it, you could say that Dad's trying to be witty. But the fact that he doesn't stop when it's apparent that his 'jokes' are a) making no one laugh and b) making everyone uncomfortable would suggest that humour isn't his primary aim.

'That's the way it should be! Sure why would men be doing it when we have women to do it for us? Women like doing it! Don't they, Emer?'

It goes on and on. Is no one going to ask him to leave me alone? I know that if I say anything it'll just make it worse. Ronan or Ciarán will tell him to give over, won't they? Dad doesn't let up. Eventually, Ronan offers:

'Oh-ho Dad, you better stop, she'll go mad!'

Great. Thanks.

'Ah, she's too sensitive – these feminists: sure everyone knows that the women do the cooking and the cleaning and the men do the real work.'

I say: 'well I never saw you do much real work to be honest, Dad. All I ever saw you do was sit around on your fucking hole.'

This is a shitty thing to say. It's cruel; it's purposefully hurtful; it's horrible. I shouldn't have said it. But, in that moment, I'm so incredibly angry. I hate them. I hate Ronan, who – at thirty – acts as though he couldn't possibly be expected to scrub an oven dish in his mother's house, who acts as though it is an insult to his superior masculine person to even be asked. I hate Ciarán, who – at twenty-six – would probably keep schtum while someone reasonably outlined their thesis as to why women should be denied the vote if it meant there wouldn't be any conflict. I hate my mum, for putting me in this situation. I hate my dad, because he's so broken when it comes to gender stuff that there's no point in even trying. I hate Saoirse, for still playing the good-girl role and propping up the system. I hate this house. I hate Ireland. I hate being made to feel like I'm the wicked witch of the fucking west for simply asking that I be treated as an equal.

I leave the room. I take the dog. She still likes me. On the way out I hear the macho mate say: 'So, Ronan, does Emer have a boyfriend?'

I don't go home again for over a year.

THE IMPOSSIBLE TASK OF IGNORING THE CRITICS

I don't hate my family. I love my family. I don't hate Ireland. I love Ireland (though it drives me spare). What I hate is patriarchy – societal gender relations based on sexism. But the hard thing is, patriarchy is made up of people I love.

I've talked a lot in this book about the tension between structure and agency – about the unanswerable question of how much of the way we act is individual choice and how much is socially determined. And I've suggested that one of the best ways to investigate this is to try to act differently and see what happens.

Butler, remember, talks about the performativity of gender roles – how, through repetition over time, gendered acts come to feel 'like us'. For the good girl I was when I was fifteen, my gender role felt like a choice. But, of course, the acts we repeat over time, that we experience as stemming from our innermost identities, have been conditioned. My fifteen-year-old self enjoyed applause for doing her gender 'right'. As an adult woman, I am regularly hissed off stage for doing my gender 'wrong'.

For Butler, to a greater or lesser degree, we are capable of performing our genders differently, of acting outside of the roles we've been given, potentially changing the system. For Pierre Bourdieu, this is rose-tinted-spectacle talk. We can't just perform ourselves into completely different ways of interacting with the social world. For one thing, we have embodied relationships with our identities; for another, the system benefits the powerful, and the powerful will lose privilege if it changes, so the system resists our attempts to act differently, by rewarding and punishing us.

This might seem a bit abstract. What nefarious overlords are punishing us for acting differently? The thing is, the way in which people protect the status quo isn't normally conscious and intentional. My brothers are not thinking 'let's reinforce the patriarchy!' when they fail to do a fair share of the labour that goes into a family occasion. They don't believe that things like housework are important, because they are the products of a system that teaches them not to value women's unpaid domestic labour. So, when asked to help, they experience nagging and bossiness – female stereotypes that are typically used to silence women when they ask for equality. And they react just like anyone would when they meet a bossy nag – they tell her to piss off.

They are, of course, strengthening a patriarchal system in which women do the vast majority of unpaid domestic labour. Their behaviour directly affects women's prospects for combining career and family and for holding positions of power: positions that might allow us to radically restructure society to account for female experience. Their behaviour indirectly disadvantages working-class women, who can't afford to either a) stay at home or b) hire a cleaner. But they don't experience their behaviour as sexist or classist. They're not *intentionally* punishing women who try to act outside sexist gender roles.

Similarly, my full-time-working mother is not thinking 'patriarchy, yay!' when she waits on us all or instructs me to serve male family members. Instead, she is a product of a system that teaches women that they show love through feeding and cleaning up after their families.

I'm telling these stories partly because discussions of structure and agency can seem a bit cold. The word structure conjures up images of concrete institutions and incomprehensible economics. But structure is family dinners. Structure is held in place by love. One huge and important reason why we women perform our gender roles is because we love people and we want to make them happy and we want them to love us back. There are definitely worse reasons to do things.

I'm also telling these stories because performing differently can be difficult in emotionally painful ways. I don't think that there is a way to act outside gender roles that will not sometimes make your loved ones uncomfortable or angry. I don't think there's a way to do it that will not make you lose it once in a while. We need to be prepared for this, to have strategies to deal with foreseeable conflicts. But, honestly, if there's a way of performing gender differently without hurting or angering those who liked the 'old' you better, please send it to me on a postcard.

Sad as it is, performing your gender differently can make those who benefit from or who serve patriarchy love you less. You are aggressive, you are naggy, you are conflict, you are difficult, you are selfish, you are complaining when other people have it so much worse, you used to be such a good girl. The audience won't stay to hear your monologue. No one will throw red roses.

People often tell feminists that we need to soften our message, to get men on board, to be sweeter. This is bull.

We're trying to dismantle male privilege and you can't sugar coat that. I have been pleading with my brothers to do a fair share of domestic labour since we were kids. Every Christmas, every family event, every time I've been home, I've drawn attention to their privilege and the sexism implicit in expecting women to serve men. Then one day I got angry. And I didn't come home for Christmas that year. I didn't come home at all. They've recognised there is a problem, and, to my sincere surprise and deep gratitude, they are trying to change.

I didn't expect this outcome. On my first trip home since the day of rotten tomatoes, Ronan and I talked about it. He said: 'when you didn't come home for Christmas, I couldn't understand why you were so angry with us. I thought: it can't really be about housework. But then I remembered back to being in school and you asking me and Ciarán to help all the time, and Mum coming home from work late, exhausted and shouting about the state of the kitchen, and Dad not doing anything – I mean, you were out of there like a flash. You turned seventeen, finished school, got a job, and whoosh. And I thought, it's probably hard for Emer to come back here and see Mum still doing all the work, and us still doing nothing.'

My big brother can be pretty great.

'But you need to explain these things to us without getting so aggressive,' he continued, 'and housework would be a stupid thing to fall out with your family over. Some people have real problems.'

He still has a way to go.

Maya Angelou says: 'each time a woman stands up for

herself, without knowing it possibly, without claiming it, she stands up for all women.' As someone who's been socialised to put the needs of others first, this helps me. I know my white, middle-class problems are tiny compared to those of so many other women. But it's all sexism, and we all have to do our best to tackle it where we find it, not only through public activism, but also in our own lives. Otherwise, regardless of what we say, what we write, or where we march, the structure will go on replicating itself.

Ultimately, I believe that it's more important to be the kind of woman who loves herself and other women enough to demand that she is treated at all times as an equal than it is to win the love of those who refuse to recognise or remedy inequality. I believe this even though it can run contrary to what I feel; I believe it even though, sometimes, it breaks my heart.

CHAPTER TWELVE:

REPRISE

'To *play means to do something that is neither "seri-ous" nor "real". Yet play is nonetheless important, for it demands risks and promises rewards that may have consequences for our everyday lives. We play to escape, to step out of everyday existence, if only for a moment, and to observe a different set of rules. We play to explore, to learn about ourselves and the world around us.'*

Henry Bial[88]

BACK BY POPULAR DEMAND

At twenty-nine, I've been practising body non-conformity in a committed way for about three years. I still love to dress up, but my outfits are often gender bendy; shaving my mousy tresses then letting them grow then shaving them again has become a modus operandi; I am, of course, a hairy feminist beastie; I have one pair of high heels that live, sad and despondent, beneath my bed; bras are optional; I don't wear make-up most of the time, but enjoy the ritual of smoky eyes when I do; I'm happy in pink; I'm happy in blue; I'm happy femme; I'm happy butch; I'm happiest androgynous; mainly, I'm just happy.

One of the things I love about how I choose to do body non-conformity is that it has drastically simplified my body routine and diminished the stress I feel about grooming. Mornings are easy. My showers take five minutes – soap and shampoo. Face cream, deodorant and toothpaste are the only other body products I use daily. I put on something comfortable and cute, smile at myself in the mirror, have a cuppa and toast, and scurry off.

When I think of how my morning routine used to go. In the shower: shampoo, conditioner, all-over loofah using body gel; shaving pits and legs using shaving foam and razor; face wash; I think at one point I even had special foot wash. Out of the shower: body lotion; eye cream; face cream; hair serum; blow dry and arrange hair in zigzag parting (because my roots are awful and I can't afford a half-head of highlights right now); eyebrow and chin twease; deodorant; foundation; concealer; eyeliner; eyeshadow; mascara; blush; powder; lip gloss. I have now achieved 'the natural look'.

Try on clothes and look in mirror. Feel fat. Change clothes. Look in mirror. Still feel fat. Change clothes. Decide that this outfit emphasises my bum (which is my best bit, you understand) and hides my tummy (which is my worst bit, you understand). Choose earrings and necklace. Check face for foundation lines or wayward mascara. Spritz perfume. Look at watch. Scream. Grab slice of bread smeared with peanut butter while running out door. Arrah shite, my nail varnish has chipped.

And that's just daily. Don't get me started on the weekly Immac of my bikini line, or fake-tan maintenance during the summer. Don't mention the constant self-consciousness and distress over the downy hair on my cheeks, upper lip and chin. And compared to friends of mine, I was really pretty low-maintenance – I never had professional waxes, manis, pedis, facials or spray tans; I only had my hair done every three or four months, and never straightened or curled it.

When I did all this stuff, I'd scoff at people who asked me how I had the time. What were they doing in the forty-five minutes it took me to get ready in the morning? Making splints for the broken legs of baby birds that had fallen from their nests? Reversing global warming? And anyway, I liked my routine of femininity. But now that my nails are clipped not filed and my skin is warm and pink instead of flat beige, I can't imagine going back to it. It's just stressful. And it never made me feel good about myself. Not really.

Another of the things I like about my body since I stopped striving to make myself the Goddess of the Beauty Myth is that it feels like I inhabit a political statement. If I turn up to work looking feminine one day and masculine the next, I'm highlighting the fact that gender is a costume, and asking those around me to treat people in the same way whether they look masculine or feminine. My hairy legs say that I believe shaming women's bodies is sexist. My shaved head asks: do you ever wonder why this is a boy's hairstyle and not a girl's hairstyle? No make-up on Monday says: I like my face. Make-up on Tuesday says: I like decorating my face. I have a sense of what my costumes symbolise and, while I can't control how I am read, I can at least try to tell the story about gender and performance that I want to tell.

But after three years, and having done a lot of work to feel comfortable in my skin, I begin to wonder what it would feel like to re-inhabit the costume of normative femininity. The ideal costume used to feel 'like me', but now my body non-conformity feels authentic. I started to imagine shaving and tanning and dyeing and all the rest, and I realised that a) to create the costume from scratch would be a pretty huge and time-consuming undertaking and b) the thought of walking around London hyper-femme actually freaked me out.

An idea for a new personal experiment in gender performativity, structure and agency was born.

I told my friend Dan about it. He laughed: 'You hold the handrail on the Tube with your massive armpit bush hanging out, but you're scared to go out looking like a pretty girl?' I laughed too, but made him promise to meet me for moral support and drinks when my transformation was complete.

THE MAKEOVER: DAY 1

My hair was very short at the time. I considered buying a wig, but wig shopping proved disastrous: I looked like a girl trying to look like a boy trying to look like a girl, which was just not the hetero-normative aesthetic I was after. I decided I'd dye my do instead, potentially fooling the world into mistaking a grown-out £7 short back and sides for a funky Toni and Guy pixie cut.

I booked into a Brixton beauty salon for an all-over body wax, eyebrow wax and spray tan. I'd never done these things before and I figured it would be interesting to experience what many other women experience as part of their beauty regimes. I bought a French manicure set, sighing, thinking of the minutes I'd have to sit there waiting for polish to dry when I could be playing guitar or tormenting the cat.

I was pretty confident I could do the dye-job myself. I've been peroxide blonde before: my friend Siobhán is a hairdresser and I'd watched her bleach my hair numerous times over the sink in my kitchen. So I bought a packet of peroxide from Boots and followed all the instructions, except for the one about doing strand tests, because no one ever bothers with that bollox. Forty minutes later I had a beautiful head of bright orange hair.

I consulted the internet. Apparently, dyeing your hair peroxide blonde is actually quite technical. Apparently, I needed something called purple toner. I ran frantically into the street, with only a bandana to cover my sunny delight coiffure, and arrived at Boots with a mass of orange peel escaping over my forehead. There was no purple toner in the hair-dye aisle, so I asked the lady at the counter to help me. She started laughing. I started laughing. After a while, I stopped laughing and waited for what seemed like a long time. Finally, she stopped too, took a deep breath, and said: 'Your hair is funny.'

Boots had no purple toner, but it had a two-tier peroxide dye set, the second part of which consisted of purple toner. So I bought that. I followed all the instructions for step two of the set perfectly, except for the bit about doing strand tests, because nobody bothers with that bullshit. The purple toner had no effect.

I returned to the annals of the internet. If the purple toner doesn't work, it's because you haven't lightened your hair sufficiently. So I used part one of the two-step peroxide system, following all the instructions to the letter, except for the bit about protecting your hairline with Vaseline and doing strand tests. It stung like crazy. After half an hour, I tried to comb through my hair and bits of it were breaking off, so I figured it was time to rinse.

My hair was now yellow. Yellow was better. I also had some quite nasty chemical burns on the side of my face, but not to worry: I could cover those up with make-up. Armed with apocryphal internet wisdom that purple toner will make yellow hair less yellow, I hit the streets of Brixton once more and finally found this elusive substance in an Afro-Caribbean beauty shop. I followed all the instructions, except how long to leave it on because surely I'd had my share of bad luck for one day.

I blowdried my hair. It was less yellow. It was also more purple. I rubbed some moisturiser into the purple bits on a whim. This kind of worked. I parted it so that the least yellow, least purple bits were on show, and ran around the house looking at myself in various lights. Give or take a yellow or purple streak or ten, I now had acceptable peroxide-blonde hair. Piece of cake.

That was enough beautification for one day.

THE MAKEOVER: DAY 2

I booked an early morning waxing appointment. At the salon, the charming beautician Aisha welcomed me and asked me to fill out a form with my name, my address, my telephone number, and my *doctor*'s name, my *doctor*'s address and my *doctor*'s telephone number. Very reassuring. Aisha was pregnant and suffering from an excess of saliva (which I didn't even know was a pregnancy symptom) so she couldn't talk much, but was excellent at making friendly noises.

I went into a nicely lit room and was asked to strip naked and lie on the massage table. I was given a towel to cover my boobs, which seemed a bit pointless. Gentle, tinkly music was playing. Candles were burning. It was all very lovely.

We started with the legs. 'How long is it since you last waxed?' Aisha asked. 'Three years,' I said, and off I rambled nervously about experiments and gender and how she's going to be in my book.

Legs. Easy. Less painful than pulling off a plaster. 'This isn't as bad as I thought it was going to be,' I said, and Aisha mmmhmm-ed knowingly, gesturing at me when it was time to turn round like a roasting chicken. I was feeling pretty smug by the time my legs were done, thinking 'I probably have quite a high pain threshold in comparison to other people. This isn't going to be bad at all.'

Armpits. More difficult. I trimmed before I came so that the hair wouldn't be too long, but having these coarse hairs ripped out by the root was nasty. Aisha got me to pull my boob in the opposite direction to her waxing strip so that the skin was taut. I watched as tiny bubbles of blood surfaced where the hair had been. Aisha dabbed them away with a cotton pad, making approving little 'mmm-hmms' to herself: her war on hair was proceeding to plan.

Vulva.

Vulva.

Vulva.

Oh my fucking God.

Aisha got me to pull my tummy upwards to create a taut surface from which to remove my upper rug. She applied the hot wax and patted it until satisfied with the consistency. Then she ripped. It felt like my skin was coming off. 'Sweet Jesus,' I screamed. Aisha made an 'mmm-hmm' that translated to 'I know, right? Painful, right?' and should probably have been construed as solidarity, but in my state I wondered if she was taunting me for my earlier hubris.

The bikini line area wasn't bad, but the outer labia were torture. There's no way to pull the skin taut – you've just got to rip. 'It'll all be worth it in the end,' Aisha braved her saliva to say, as I struggled to breathe through the burning, tearing sensation engulfing the most sensitive part of my body. How would anything be worth this? But I had no time to voice my misgivings, because she was ripping wax from the other side, creating a pain so intense that I laughed maniacally and shouted: 'Women are so brave! We are so brave!'

Aisha made her roly-poly chicken gesture again and I spun onto my front. Then she mimed parting curtains, and it took me a second to understand that I was supposed to reach backwards and hold my butt cheeks open in her honour. Having your crack denuded is most unpleasant, but after you've had your labia all but torn off nothing's going to shock you. Except maybe the dollop of wax on your actual asshole. I'll just repeat that: on your actual asshole.

Aisha exited, leaving some moisturiser for my newly-naked intimates. I rubbed it in, thinking 'there there little vulva, there there little outer labia, there there little arsehole. It'll never happen again.' There was a mirror in the room and I looked at myself, arms raised, pudenda poised. Aside from the fact that everything was red and sore, the last time I'd seen my body looking like this was when I was 13 years old, and I couldn't help but observe that there was something very childlike, very vulnerable, about the pink clamshell of skin tucked between my thighs.

That was enough beautification for one day.

THE MAKEOVER: DAY 3

Aisha welcomed me back. Her pregnancy symptoms persisted. We began with a consultation on how I'd like my eyebrows. I said I'd like them to match. I gathered from Aisha's own eyebrow action that this wasn't what she meant, so I left it to her discretion. During the heat and pain bit, my vanity kicked in, because my natural eyebrows are really quite nice, and I was worried that this was going to leave me with pinched little strips.

When I looked in the mirror I was relieved. Aisha's sculptoral efforts left my wee caterpillars quite close to the originals. Except now they matched (just like I asked!) and I looked decidedly more like a vulcan. It's life, Jim, but instead of soft curves and blurred boundaries, instead of spectrums, instead of anomalies, instead of the incoherence of the body, it's geometric lines, it's precision, it's order. I would have stayed there and had philosophical thoughts about the human desire to create order from chaos and how that affects our gender identities and our relationships with our bodies, but it was time for my spray tan.

I donned a pair of disposable knickers and stood in a tall three-sided tent. Aisha entered with something that looked like it had been borrowed from the props table of *Rambo* – the AK47 of tanning – and mimed at me to assume various positions as she blasted. Afterwards, I was given a hoover hose that pumped out hot air and stood in the tent blow-drying myself for what was apparently ten minutes but felt like a decade because blow-drying yourself is excruciatingly boring.

Enough beautification.

REVEAL

It was evening. I made up my face meticulously, styled my dubiously dyed hair, zipped myself into a little red dress (from New Look, naturally) and, after performing an in-expert French manicure on my toes in order to create the fashionable illusion of having very long, very clean toe-nails, I dug my stilettos out from under the bed and thus my transformation was complete. My friend Fliss took some pictures for posterity, then, with the aid of wine, I psyched myself up for a trip into town to meet my friends in a bar.

On the Tube, I felt self-conscious, as though I was in outlandish drag. I wanted to explain to strangers: 'This isn't what I look like.' I missed the awareness that my body was a kind of political symbol, that it said something about what I believe and who I am. If my body said anything now, it wasn't a lecture I wanted to give. I felt sure that people *must* be staring at me: I'd undergone so many bizarre, painful and time-consuming processes to look this way. But here's the thing – they weren't.

No one was staring. My hair, now a cartoonish shade of blonde, was held in place with wax and spray; there was no way that my uniformly bronze skin was the product of a London summer or a week's holiday; my lips were blood red, my eyes kohl-lined, my eyebrows geometric lines; my legs and underarms were inhumanly shiny and smooth; I was wearing a bra that modified my bustline, hiding my nipples and making my chest look bigger; I had four-inch spikes strapped to my ankles; the nails at my extremities had been varnished to create an illusion of impossible length and whiteness. And after all these strange, skin-burning, hair-tearing, contour-disguising, technicolour modifications, I was simply normal. No one looked twice.

When I go about my day in shorts, no bra and no make-up, in shoes that help rather than hinder my mobility, with skin that's a habitual shade of pink: people routinely stare and whisper. Once, in a Tube carriage just like that one, I heard a group of girls speaking *as Gaelige* (in Irish) and was about to join in, explaining that I'm from Galway and asking how they were enjoying London, when I realised that, thinking I couldn't understand, they were talking about the hair on my legs. I've even caught strangers surreptitiously taking pictures of me. And as I clocked this, I felt a lump in my throat, because the relationship between our bodies and our society is so deeply messed up.

WHAT'S THE MORAL OF THE STORY?

My experiment in gender performativity, structure and agency was a visceral reminder of just how socially unacceptable the unmodified female body has become. And it taught me some other things besides.

I spent the next few weeks trying to inhabit a normatively feminine physicality again, and was surprised by how complicated it was. I'd forgotten how to factor time for modifications into the day, and I hated constantly running for the Tube, slice of toast half in hand, half in gob. I no longer liked the feeling of wearing heavy make-up – the niggling worry that there was mascara-smudge under my eyes was annoying.

Positively, I found that I'd trained myself out of the aesthetic opinion that I look better with make-up. This came as a surprise – I used to wear make-up every single day; at one point I felt as though I couldn't leave the house without it. But now, when I looked in the mirror at my ruddy complexion first thing, I realised I liked the softness of it, the life of it, and I felt quite loath to airbrush myself into the stiffness and starkness of beige skin and darkened eyelashes. When I did, instead of the improvement I used to see, I just saw change. I didn't look better, just different. While I still enjoy the ritual of powder and paint on a Friday night or special occasion, I've grown to love the before picture better. And that really does make me happy.

The legacy of my Hollywood wax convinced me that this particular facet of female grooming is batshit. There were about three days of smoothness after the plucked-chicken effect faded, then I started to get a rash. Soon, my entire vulva was covered with small, angry pimples. Anytime I walked anywhere it itched, and during the first week of my new job in Canada, I had to keep sneaking to the loo for a quick scratch. I'd get home in the evening, tear my knickers off and pat the poor mangey beast with cold water. I asked other women who'd had Hollywoods if they'd experienced anything similar, and a few casually said, 'Oh yeah, that does happen when it's growing out alright, yeah.' What? How is maddening itch and hideous rash an acceptable side effect of fanny waxing? Who finds the mange aesthetic sexier than pubic hair? Are we living in a society of poxophiles?

But, overall, the sad truth is that, scratchy pants and missed breakfasts notwithstanding, after a day or two of mental re-adjustment, inhabiting a normative gendered costume was just so much easier than my regular day-to-day.

When I met my friends on that first evening in London, there were shrieks and howls of disbelief. But there were plenty of compliments too. 'Am I allowed to say that you look great?' asked the lovely Henry. And, as drinks helped me to relax into costume, I started to enjoy things. There's an undeniable pleasure in turning a head or two on the way to the ladies, and knowing it's not because you're a hairy-legged skinhead wearing a 'Kiss Me I'm Palestinian' T-shirt.

The next day, when I raised my arm to wave at a friend across the street, I found that the gesture was accompanied by a quick pang of anxiety. Then I remembered: 'Oh, but it's okay, I'm shaved at the moment.' I realised that the simple, everyday gesture of raising my arm above my head had been causing me mild anxiety every day for three years. So much so that the gesture itself evoked the emotion, even in the absence of body hair. I'd become so used to the feeling of discomfort that I'd ceased to even notice I was experiencing it.

Wearing summer dresses was easier. Meeting new people was easier. I got male attention again – most of it awful, but some quite nice. A man in a copy-shop wouldn't let me pay for my printing because I was 'so sweet'. It was a relief that at a time in which I was starting a new job in a new country, I didn't have to worry about what my colleagues, students, neighbours, dates or new friends thought.

It felt as though I'd given myself a little holiday from feminist activism through body non-conformity. A break that I probably needed – both to get some perspective on my experiences and to give me back a little of the angst I felt when I started practising it. I thought I had done all the work, that my attempts to break down my gendered conditioning in relation to my body had been successful, but the ease with which I could undo all that effort, and the sheer mental release of not inhabiting a socially transgressive physicality showed me that I might have opened the cage door, but I hadn't flown the cage. Oh Pierre Bourdieu, you are more right about the durability of the habitus than I want you to be.

Gradually, I chopped the blonde out of my hair, allowed my body hair to return, and went back to switching between masculine and feminine costumes at will. It was much easier to feel comfortable in my non-normativity the second time. But I will always know how my society codes men and women, how it expects them to behave, and how disgusted it is by women who don't conform. This knowledge is part of my identity, and I can't get rid of it.

Perhaps this is what makes performing differently so powerful – the consciousness it gives you of how your beliefs conflict with your emotions, of how much of the way you think and act is not really voluntary. This awareness, for me, has been a great source of strength as I try – not always succeeding – to act differently. The more I want to live in a world in which it isn't so difficult to perform my gender freely, the more I strive to create that world.

IN PLAY

Sometimes (okay, often) when I describe my experiments in gender performativity, people ask, 'What does all this accomplish?' I come up against the idea that to be efficacious or worthwhile, feminist activism – whether personal or collective – must be stony-faced and grave. More than one friend has expressed exasperated disbelief that I actually think I'm effecting any change with this kind of play. 'Are you serious?' they say, 'you're chipping away at patriarchy by having your arse waxed and thinking about how it makes you feel?'

Well, when you put it like that.

Am I serious? I'm playfully serious. I'm seriously playful.

The concept of play is a strange and fascinating one. Humans, as I pointed out in Chapter Four, like to imagine that there's a clear line between truth and fiction, between reality and representation. By this kind of logic, fictions and representations are human made: they are not true or real, but part of our shared cultural imagination.

At first glance, play might seem to belong strictly to the realm of fiction or representation. But, as the theorist Johan Huzinga points out, humans are not the only animals that play – many animals do: watch fox cubs mock-fighting, or dolphins cavorting. Play is not just something belonging to human culture, but something that precedes it. This pretending, this performance, this fun: it's not a rational thing.[89]

Yet, we can't just call it instinct. Human play is clearly not instinct – a football match, a game of tag, a theatre performance, two children playing doctor – we learn how to do all of these things within a cultural system. Huzinga says: 'in acknowledging play you acknowledge mind, for whatever else play is, it is not matter.' He means that, in playing, we create another reality – a shared, symbolic space – alongside the world of nature.

Play, then, is a paradox: it shows at once that human culture is not rational, yet that we can intentionally use the mind to shape our world. Play is silly. Play is subversive.

It muddies the line between representation and reality; it shows that there's truth in fiction, and fiction in truth.

So I pretend not to notice when people roll their eyes at my attention to performance, my serious consideration of the playful things in life: at my hunt for gender-neutral toys; or critiques of gender stereotypes in cartoons; at my cross-dressing; or genderbending; or predilection for nude art projects; or makeovers; or hairy legs; or refusal to tell them whether my friends are girls or boys; or my ridicule of media representations of sex; or my tacky sexuality (which can't be taken seriously).

Play is a tool that at once exposes the irrational underpinnings of our unequal culture, and allows us to imagine new possibilities into being. And it's so much fun. And it's so much more. Because when we laugh at someone who's playing with our social expectations, we know, at heart, that they are laughing at everything that would justify our mirth.

CONCLUSION:

FINAL CURTAIN CALL

'In one word, states of character arise out of like activities. This is why the activities we exhibit must be of a certain kind; it is because the states of character correspond to the differences between these. It makes no small difference, then, whether we form habits of one kind or of another from our very youth; it makes a very great difference, or rather all the difference.'

Aristotle[90]

DENOUEMENT

It's 327 BC, and I've decided to return to Athens, on my now considerably less spindly legs, to have another word with Aristotle. I find him sitting at the foot of the Acropolis, looking pensive, as befits a great philosopher. He snaps out of his reverie as I approach, and it takes him a moment to recognise me. 'Ah Emer,' he says, stroking his luscious beard, 'pray excuse me – I was just thinking about lunch. It is nice to see you again after all this time. It has been fourteen years, has it not? And I must say, you look less as though an enthusiastic eructation would blow you away. The childbearing years must have given you strength.'

'I don't have kids yet, actually,' I answer. 'Women tend to start families later in my time, and anyways, I'm still trying to figure out a familial and romantic structure in which I might be able to raise gender-liberated children.' 'Ah – have you read my *Politics*? I think you'll find it details the best way to structure men's roles, women's roles and families.' 'Yeah, friend Aristotle, a lot of shit changes in two millennia, you know? Your idea that some people are natural slaves? Pretty unfashionable in the future. The Hellenic conception of romantic love and sexual desire? Completely revamped. And, in the future, scientific evidence – as opposed to biased male perception – shows women and men to be intellectual equals, and women are fighting to create a world in which their social roles are not dependent on their sexed bodies.'

Aristotle laughs. 'These are very good jokes, Emer,' he says, 'but enough of the funnies, why have you travelled, once again, from the future to speak to me?' I explain: 'Aristotle, I've spent the last few years of my life reflecting on why women in my time are locked into gendered ways of behaving. I've spent much of that time trying to act differently, to see what I can learn.' 'Easy!' says the lovable sexist sage, 'I have already solved this one too! In women the deliberative capacity lacks force – they are ruled by their emotions, and men by their reason.' 'Okay Archie, but let's imagine for a moment – I know it'll be hard – that you are wrong, and that women and men are, in fact, very psychologically similar: why would women continue to act out gender identities that emphasise their physical difference from men, create the illusion of significant psychological difference, and ultimately disadvantage them? 'Hmmmm,' the philosopher ponders, ever willing to partake in a thought experiment, however frivolous: 'they must believe, at some level, that these actions will make them happy.'

There's obviously truth to this. In the seventies, as I discussed in Chapter Three, Sandra Bem's sex role inventory upended the idea that psychological well-being and social adjustment were related to conformity to the 'correct' characteristics for one's sex. But the legacy of this long-standing belief that the happiest people are girly girls and manly men lives on. If people fail to conform to gender norms – if, for example, women choose not to remove their moustaches or men decide to wear dresses – they tend to be read as weird, mixed-up, even unstable. So there's a degree to which performing your gender according to society's prescriptions protects you from judgement and harm, and, you could argue that avoiding this unhappiness constitutes a striving for happiness.

Judith Butler told us that gender identity is performative – that it is constructed through a stylised repetition of acts over time. But we don't create our own stylised repetitions from scratch. We inherit a set of norms – a script – from history and from the culture that surrounds us. Butler notes that people are rewarded in many ways for performing their gender identities 'correctly'. If you costume and comport yourself according to your society's ideal of femininity, you get benefits: you might be considered more sexually attractive, or trustworthy, or lovable.

Equally, there are repercussions – even violent repercussions – to performing your gender incorrectly. Butler talks about the death of Charlie Howard: a teenager beaten up, thrown over a bridge and killed by his classmates because he had an effeminate walk. She asks why a boy with an effeminate walk is capable of creating the kind of anxiety that leads to murder, and says that this case, like so many others, must make us acknowledge that coercion is a big part of why we conform to gender norms.

In an awareness of this system of rewards and punishments, you could say that conforming to gender norms is a way of ensuring greater happiness. But, of course, conforming in order to gain advantages or prevent suffering within a system that values women in disempowering ways does nothing to change the system. Sure, you gain a certain amount of confidence from performing a domestically-inclined, sweet, unconfrontational, conventionally costumed and physically conditioned ideal, but the kind of happiness resulting from this is not the kind of happiness that might result from a world that valued people in male and female bodies equally; it's not the kind of happiness that might result from being valued in terms of your personality, your talents, your unique beauty, your goodness, your self.

'Aristotle,' I say, 'I don't think it's enough to argue that women perform like this because it makes them happy. In fact, if the ultimate end is happiness, I think this performance of womanhood stops us from ever attaining it. The little fulfillment we derive from our conformity puts the great fulfillment we could achieve through our non-conformity forever out of reach. It's like being hungry on the way to a beautiful banquet and stuffing your face with a bumper bag of stale Doritos you found down the back of the passenger seat.' Aristotle doesn't know what Doritos are, but he is quite hungry, and my talk of a banquet encourages him to wander off for lunch.

Part of the reason that we're locked into disempowering systems of behaviour is that we experience our thoughts, feelings and behaviours as choices (agency), even when they are largely the products of a subtly coercive system (structure). I've returned to this tension throughout *Girls Will Be Girls*. However, another reason why I think we uphold gender roles is because it's hard to imagine alternatives. Repeating the behaviours we see all around us, from the script we have inherited, is easy; writing our own scripts takes effort. But it's also more fulfilling (in Aristotle's sense) and more fun (in Cyndi Lauper's).

I hope this book has begun to suggest some alternatives that you can play with in ways that feel right for you. Whether it's nurturing the next generation of little starlets by providing them with good scripts, good props and, of course, an inspirational leading lady; whether it's analysing the art that surrounds you, becoming aware of how much of the literature, film, TV and theatre you consume is about women or by women, and working to surround yourself and others with other, more equal texts; whether it's thinking through the structure that's moulded how we experience our agency, and striving to break down the sexist, racist, classist ablest assumptions that are embedded in all of our psychologies; whether it's wearing a cunning disguise at Halloween or genderbending in 'real' life, thus shaking up a symbolic system built on binary gender; whether it's examining your performative gender identity and its relationship with your biological sex; whether it's challenging taboos on the female body or finding revolutionary ways to be beautiful; whether it's hairy armpits or gender neutral language; whether it's hot, non-binary sex acts or proud non-binary sexualities; whether it's refusing to play house or agreeing to play an unconventional social role; and even if it's none of these things, I hope you've found something here that you can take out into the world to create the change you want to see.

I believe our performances will have a happy ending. Because underlying gender inequality in our society is the erroneous but widely held belief that men and women are more different to each other in their abilities, psychological characteristics and emotions than they are from members of the same sex. This belief is upheld by the ways in which we perform our genders. Using your body and behaviours to destabilise the social constructions of masculinity and femininity that so many of us have accepted as inevitable is a crucial political and ethical gesture.

If we're acting in ways that, deep down, we don't believe are right – because this is what we've been conditioned to do – then we're never really going to be fulfilled. The only happiness we'll get is from receiving rewards or avoiding punishments within a system that we don't respect. It's kind of like dating someone you don't like just because they like you. We need to create a society that respects and values all people equally: this means highlighting the arbitrary cultural divisions between men and women in our society; it means giving everyone real freedom to act outside of the gender role deemed appropriate to their biological sex. And it means that girls can change the world with the ways they choose to be girls.

ACKNOWLEDGEMENTS

Thanks to my agent, Juliet Pickering, without whom there would be no *Girls Will Be Girls*. She encouraged and advised me every step of the way. Thanks also to all at Blake Friedmann, for feedback, support and prosecco. Special mentions to Victoria Innell (good cop) and Hattie Grünewald (bad cop) for reading chapters as I wrote, and offering valuable opinions.

Thanks to my exceptional editor, Jane Sturrock, who commissioned *Girls Will Be Girls*, and who serves her insightful criticism straight up, just the way I like it. Her no-punch-pulling editorial style was exactly what I needed to write this book. Thanks also to all at Orion, especially Emma Smith, who was such an invaluable help in finding the title.

Thanks to Holly Baxter and Rhiannon Lucy Cosslett of *The Vagenda*, for creating the platform on which my writing was first noticed. Thanks to all the staff at *The Guardian Comment is Free*, especially Jessica Reed and Maya Wolfe-Robinson, for commissioning me and encouraging my work.

Thanks to my first draft readers, Breanna Morrison, Sarah Haberl, Deirdre Troy (my bestie) and Alice Cahill. Thanks especially to Dr Susan Cahill and Raymond Rollin, who sat down and went through the manuscript with me, page by page.

Thanks to Dr Kristen Dunfield and Dr Meera Paleja, for their advice on the section on schema; to Dr Felicity Gee, for her help with the intersex material; to Dr Melanie Racette-Campbell for endless information on sexuality in the ancient world; to Dr Mireille McLaughlin for resources on gender and language; and to Dr Daniel O'Gorman, for sending me a list of 138 slang words for boobs.

Thanks to my family. Especially Mum. I know I'm not easy. I love you.

Thanks to Prof. Helen Gilbert, first my PhD co-supervisor and then my boss, for giving me flexible working hours while I was trying to secure a deal for this book, and for being an excellent role model generally. Thanks to Dr Karen Fricker, also my PhD co-supervisor: she taught me how to think good, and her accessible academia on funky subjects is ever an inspiration.

Thanks to my colleagues at the School of Canadian Irish studies, Concordia University, for providing a supportive environment in which to write. Michael, Rhona, Gavin, Matina, Ruth, Jane, Susan (again!), Gearóid and Seaghan – I'm so lucky to work with you. Thanks to my Performance Studies students of Winter 2014, who were guinea pigs for much of this material.

Thanks to my flatmate, Byron Taylor-Conboy, for making writing from home a lovely experience. Thanks to my ex-flatmates, Sophie Johnson, Jack Deacon and Chris Pepler, for keeping me sane(ish) through the surreal period of my life where I was famous for having hairy armpits.

To all my cherished friends and relations in Galway, Dublin, London, Montréal and further afield: love and gratitude.

And, last but very certainly not least, thanks to you, for reading this book. I hope you liked it.

ENDNOTES

1 Butler, Judith. 'Performative acts and gender constitution: An essay in phenomenology and feminist theory.' Theatre journal (1988): 519–531. p. 526

2 Duggan, Lisa, and Kathleen McHugh. 'A Fem (me) inist Manifesto.' *Women & Performance: A Journal of Feminist Theory* 8.2 (1996): 153–159. p. 154

3 Hanna, Kathleen. 'Riot Grrrl Manifesto.' *Bikini Kill* Zine 2 (1991). p. 2

4 Aristotle. *Nicomachean Ethics*. Trans. WD Ross. Kitchener: Batoche, 1999. Book 2, Ch 1.

5 'the slave has no deliberative faculty at all; the woman has, but it is without authority, and the child has, but it is immature. So it must necessarily be supposed to be with the moral virtues also; all should partake of them, but only in such manner and degree as is required by each for the fulfill-ment of his duty. Hence the ruler ought to have moral virtue in perfection, for his function, taken absolutely, demands a master artificer, and rational principle is such an artificer; the subjects, on the other hand, require only that measure of virtue which is proper to each of them. Clearly, then, moral virtue belongs to all of them; but the temperance of a man and of a woman, or the courage and justice of a man and

of a woman, are not, as Socrates maintained, the same; the courage of a man is shown in commanding, of a woman in obeying.' Aristotle, *Politics* 1.8

6 I've borrowed this use of the utterance 'it's a girl' from Judith Butler's *Bodies that Matter*. See: Butler, Judith, *Bodies that Matter: On the Discursive Limits of Sex*, 1993, Routledge (2011): p. 177

7 See: Fine, Cordelia, *Delusions of Gender: The Real Science Behind Sex Difference*, Icon (2010): particularly pp. 189–213

8 See: Hutchinson, Nicky and Chris Calland, *Body Image in the Primary School*, Routledge (2011): pp. 8–9

9 Thompson, T. L., & Zerbinos, E., 'Gender Roles in Animated Cartoons: Has the Picture Changed in 20 Years?', *Sex Roles*, 32 (1995): pp. 651–674

10 Thompson, T. L., & Zerbinos, E., 'Television Cartoons: Do Children Notice it's a Boy's World?' *Sex Roles*, 37 (1997): pp. 415–432

11 Leaper, Campbell, Lisa Breed, Laurie Hoffman and Carly Ann Pearlman, 'Variations in the Gender Stereotyped Content of Children's Television Cartoons Across Genres', *Journal of Applied Social Psychology*, 32.8 (2002): pp. 1653–1662

12 Harrison, Kristen and Nicole Martins, 'Racial and Gender Differences in the Relationship Between Children's TV Use and Self-Esteem: A Longitudinal Panel Study', *Communications Research*, 39.3 (2012): pp. 338–57

13 Wā Thiong'o, Ngũgĩ, *Decolonizing the Mind: The Politics of Language in African Literature*, 1986, East African Educational Pub (2004)

14 Dollimore, Jonathan. *Radical Tragedy*. Brighton: Harvester, 1984; University of Chicago Press, 1984. p. 25

15 If you're interested in learning more about structure and agency, as well as related sociological concepts, Anthony Gidden's work is rigorous but accessible. Maybe begin with Giddens, Anthony, *Sociology (7th Edition)*, Cambridge: Polity (2013)

16 Scarman, Sir Leslie George, *The Scarman Report: the Brixton Disorders, 10–12 April 1981,* London: Her Majesty's Stationary Office (1981)

17 Browne, James, 'The Impact of Tax and Benefit Reforms by Sex: Some Simple Analysis', Institute of Fiscal Studies, Economic and Social Research Council (2011)

18 Randerson, James, 'World's Richest 1% Own 40% of All Wealth, UN Report Discovers', *Guardian,* 6 Dec 2006

19 Stewart, Heather, 'Shocking Figs Reveal Growth in UK's Wealth Gap', *Guardian,* 10 Feb 2013; Hadda, Moussa, (2012), 'The Perfect Storm: Economic Stagnation, the Rising Cost of Living, Public Spending Cuts, and the Impact on UK Poverty', Oxfam

20 Levine, Linda, 'An Analysis of Distribution of Wealth Across Households, 1989–2010', Congressional Research Service Report for Congress (2012)

21 Institute for Public Policy Research (2013), 'Great Expectations: Exploring the Promises of Gender Equality'

22 Milkie, Melissa, Sara B. Raley and Suzanne M. Bianchi, 'Taking on the Second Shift: Time Allocations and Time Pressures of US Parents and Preschoolers', *Social Forces* 88.2 (2009): pp. 487–517

23 See: Bakhtin, Mikhail, *Rabelais and His World* (1965), Trans. Hélène Iswolsky, Indiana UP: (2009)

24 See 'The Master Slave Dialectic', a famous passage of Hegel's

Phenomenology of Spirit, 1807. Available free from several sources online.

25 Hooks, Bell, *Feminism is for Everybody: Passionate Politics*, Cambridge: South End Press (2000): 3

26 If you'd like to learn more about implicit bias, I think this article is excellent and very accessible compared to a lot of the social science out there:
Kane, Jerry and Kristin Lane, 'Seeing Through Colourblindness: Implicit Bias and the Law', *UCLA Law Review* 59 (2010): pp. 465–520

27 See: Barlow, Rich, 'BU Research: A Riddle Reveals Depth of Gender Bias', *BU Today*, 16 Jan 2014

28 For some exciting work on what we might begin to do about this problem, you might like: Kane, Jerry et al., 'Implicit Bias in the Courtroom', *UCLA Law Review* 58 (2012): pp. 1124–1184

29 See: Bem, Sandra L., *The Lenses of Gender: Transforming the Debate on Sexual Inequality*, Yale UP (1993)

30 Bem, Sandra L., (1974), 'The Measurement of Psychological Androgyny', *Journal of Consulting and Clinical Psychology*, 42.2, pp. 155–62

31 Bem, Sandra L., *An Unconventional Family*, Yale UP (1998)

32 Wolf, Naomi, *The Beauty Myth: How Images of Beauty Are Used Against Women*, London: Vintage (1991): p. 19

33 Except for Rollin.

34 Hooks, Bell, *Feminist Theory: From Margin to Centre*. South End Press (1984); Hooks, Bell, *Feminism is for Everybody: Passionate Politics*, South End Press (2000)

35 Shildrick, Margrit and Janet Price. 'Breaking the Boundaries

of the Broken Body.' *Body & Society* 2.4 (1996): 93–113. p. 111

36 Gabler, Neal, 'Life the Movie', *The Performance Studies Reader* (2004), Henry Bial ed., Routledge (2007), pp. 76–77

37 If you'd like to learn more about postmodernism, I love Jim Powell's illustrated guide, *Postmodernism for Beginners*, which is fun, clever and lays out the genesis, theorists and artists of the movement in much more detail than I had room for here. See: Powell, Jim, *Postmodernism For Beginners*, For Beginners Books (1998)

38 Fine, Cordelia, *Delusions of Gender: The Real Science Behind Sex Differences* (2010), Icon (2012): pp. 207–208

39 Birke, Lynda. 'Bodies and biology.' Feminist Theory and the Body. Ed. Janet Price and Margrit Shildrick. Edinburgh UP, 1999. 42–49. p. 42

40 Gatens, Moira, 'Power, Bodies and Difference', *Destabilising Theory*, M Barrett and A Phillips eds., Cambridge: Polity Press (1992): p. 228

41 Intersex Society of North America, 'How Common is Intersex', ISNA.org

42 Gleghorn, Charlotte, 'Myth and the Monster of Intersex: Narrative Strategies of Otherness in Lucía Puenzo's *XXY*', *Latin American Cinema* (2011): pp. 147–72

43 Goffman, Erving, *The Presentation of the Self in Everyday Life*, Anchor (1959)

44 De Beauvoir, Simone, *The Second Sex* (1949) Trans. Constance Borde and Sheila Malovany-Chevallier, Vintage (2011)

45 Butler, Judith, 'Performative Acts and Gender Constitution: An Essay in Phenomenology and Feminist Theory', *Theatre Journal* (1988): pp. 519–531

46 Butler, Judith, *Bodies that Matter: On the Discursive Limits of Sex*, 1993, Routledge (2011): p. 177

47 This percentage of women with 'unwanted' facial hair is reported in an article on *BBC News Health* by Jane Elliot, dated 12 June 2010, as well as in a *Guardian* piece by Julie Bindell dating from August 2010. Speaking in support of the 'We Can Face It' awareness-raising campaign for women with unwanted facial hair, Dr Dawn Harper of Channel 4's *Embarrassing Bodies* also said that the problem affects approximately 40 per cent of women. However, try as I might, I can't find a study to back up this percentage. Perhaps this is because 'unwanted' facial hair isn't a very scientific category: do bushy eyebrows count? Do downy cheeks? Do a few wiry chin fellas? I feel reasonably confident using the stat, if only because *Embarrassing Bodies* must have a research team with better funding and medical expertise than I.

It was much easier to find science on the prevalence of 'excessive' facial hair, otherwise know as hirsutism. The *Embarrassing Bodies* team says that it affects up to 15 per cent of UK women. I found numerous studies that placed it around that figure. But because it's impossible to say what 'excessively' hairy is, it varied considerably, with the highest estimate I found saying that 22.1 per cent of women had excessive facial hair (See: Catherine Marin DeUgarte, K. S. Woods, Alfred A. Bartolucci and Ricardo Azziz, 'Degree of Facial and Body Terminal Hair Growth in Unselected Black and White Women: Toward a Populational Definition of Hirsutism', *The Journal of Clinical Endocrinology & Metabolism* 91.4 (2006): pp. 1345–1350). And so, if 'unwanted' facial hair affects two-fifths of all women, and 'excessive' facial hair affects up to one-fifth, when are we going to stop pathologising it? Female facial hair is normal. There's nothing wrong with it. What's wrong is how we're made to feel about it.

48 See: Rod J. Rohrich, M.D., Richard Y. Ha, M.D., Jeffrey M. Kenkel, M.D., and William P. Adams, Jr, M.D., 'Classification and Management of Gynecomastia: Defining the Role of Ultrasound-Assisted Liposuction.' *Plastic and Reconstructive Surgery* 111.2 (2003): pp. 909–932

Yup, male breast tissue: also normal.

49 Sedghi, Ami, 'UK Plastic Surgery Statistics 2012', *Guardian Datablog*, 28 Jan 2013

50 Bem, Sandra L., *The Lenses of Gender: Transforming the Debate on Sexual Inequality*, Yale (1993) pp. 30–37

51 Bem, Sandra Lipsitz. *The Lenses of Gender: Transforming the Debate on Sexual Inequality*. Yale UP: 1993. p. 5

52 Clupper, Wendy, 'The Erotic Politics of *Critical Tits*: Exhibitionism or Feminist Statement?' *Political Performances: Theory and Practice*, Susan C. Haedicke et al. Rodopi (2009) pp. 251–267

53 For an excellent further comment on male objectification and the Diet Coke advert, see: Bates, Laura, *Everyday Sexism*, Simon & Schuster (2014) pp. 309–319

54 Wolf, Naomi, *The Beauty Myth*, Vintage (1990)

55 Sedghi, Ami, 'UK Cosmetic Surgery Stats, 2013', *Guardian*, 3 Feb 2014

56 Davis, Kathy, *Reshaping the Female Body: The Dilemma of Cosmetic Surgery*, Routledge (1995)

57 Davis, Kathy, *Dubious Equalities and Embodied Differences: Cultural Studies on Cosmetic Surgeries*, Rowman & Littlefield (2003): p. 114

58 For a thorough explanation as to why, see: Baxter, Holly and Rhiannon Lucy Cosslet, *The Vagenda: A Zero Tolerance Guide to the Media*, Square Peg (2014)

59 Hooks, Bell, *Feminism is for Everybody: Passionate Politics*, South End Press (2000) p. 36

60 Lesnik-Oberstein, Karín. 'The Last Taboo: Women, Body Hair and Feminism.' *The Last Taboo: Women and Body Hair*. Ed. Karín Lesnik-Oberstein. Manchester UP, 2006. 1–17. p. 1.

61 Riordan, Teresa, *Inventing Beauty: A History of the Innovations That Have Made us Beautiful*, Random House (2004)

62 Hansen, Kristen, *Hair or Bare? The History of American Women and Hair Removal, 1914–34*, Barnard.edu (2007)

63 Bourdieu never absolutely defines the habitus, but I've found pp. 53–67 of *Logic of Practice* particularly helpful in understanding it. However, *Logic of Practice* is written in very challenging language, and if you're interested in learning more about Bourdieu's sociology, I'd recommend starting with the more accessible *Distinction*. At least, that's what I did. See: Bourdieu, Pierre, *Distinction: A Social Critique of the Judgement of Taste*, Trans. Richard Nice, Harvard: Routledge (1986); And: *The Logic of Practice*, Trans. Richard Nice, California: Stanford UP (1980)

64 Bourdieu is not particularly generous to Butler's early formulation of gender performativity, saying that the parodic performances she suggests 'probably expect too much for the meagre and uncertain results they obtain.' Burn. See: Bourdieu, Pierre, *Masculine Domination*, Stanford UP (1998)

65 Hot zombie Bourdieu is right. In her 1990 book, *Gender Trouble*, Butler implies that performing differently has the power to change embodied norms, and, by extension, social

structures. However, in her 1993 publication, *Bodies That Matter*, she stresses how much our choices and our agency are constrained by structure. She never becomes as deterministic as Bourdieu though. See: Butler, Judith, *Gender Trouble*, New York: Routledge (1990); *Bodies that Matter: On the Discursive Limits of Sex*, New York: Routledge (1993)

66 Lorde, Audrey. 'The Transformation of Silence into Language and Action.' *Sister Outsider: Essays and Speeches*. Ten Speed Press, 1984; 2007. 40–44. p. 43.

67 See: Moss-Racusin, Corinne A., et al., 'Science Faculty's Subtle Gender Biases Favor Male Students', Proceedings of the National Academy of Sciences 109.41 (2012): pp. 16474–16479

68 See: Bertrand, Marianne, and Sendhil Mullainathan, 'Are Emily and Greg More Employable than Lakisha and Jamal? A Field Experiment on Labor Market Discrimination.' No. w9873, National Bureau of Economic Research (2003)

69 Austin, J.L., *How To Do Things With Words* (1955) Oxford UP: (1962)

70 For a wonderful feminist comment on this grammar issue, see Anne Fadiman, 'The His'er Problem' in her extraordinary collection of essays, *Ex Libris*.

71 Wittgenstein, Ludwig, *Philosophical Investigations* (1953), Wiley-Blackwell (2010)

72 Carter, Angela. *The Sadean Woman and the Ideology of Pornography*. New York: Pantheon, 1978. p. 17

73 Doidge, Norman, 'Brain Scans of Porn Addicts: What's Wrong With This Picture', *Guardian*, 26 Sept 2013

74 Hite, Shere, *The Hite Report: A Nationwide Study of Female Sexuality* (1976), New York: Dell (1981)

75 O'Connell, Helen E., 'Anatomy of the Clitoris', *The Journal of Urology* 174 (2005): pp. 1189–95

76 Fisher, T. D., Moore, Z. T. and Pittenger, M. J., 'Sex on the Brain? An Examination of Frequency of Sexual Cognitions as a Function of Gender, Erotophilia, and Social Desirability', *Journal of Sex Research* (2011)

77 Cameron, Deborah, *The Myth of Mars and Venus: Do Men and Women Really Speak Different Languages?* Oxford UP (2007): particularly Chapter Eight

78 Levy, Ariel, *Female Chauvinist Pigs: Women and the Rise of Raunch Culture*, Free Press (2005): pp. 46–74

79 Hooks, Bell, *Feminism is for Everyone: Passionate Politics*, South End (2000): pp. 87–92

80 Foucault, Michel. *The History of Sexuality, Volume 1.* (1976), Vintage (1978): p. 20

81 Graves, Jenny, 'An Evolutionary View of "Gay Genes"', *Latrobe.edu.au*, 6 June 2014

82 Foucault, Michel, *The History of Sexuality, Volume 1* (1976), Vintage (1978)

83 Katz, Jonathan, *The Invention of Heterosexuality*, Chicago UP (1995)

84 Katz, Jonathan. *The Invention of Heterosexuality.* Chicago UP (1995): p. 14

85 Scott, Joan W., 'Fantasy Echo: History and the Construction of Identity', *Critical Inquiry* (2001): pp. 284–304

86 Halberstam, Judith/Jack, 'F2M: The Making of Female Masculinity' (1994) *A Feminist Theory and the Body: A Reader*. Janet Price and Margrit Shildrick eds., Edinburgh UP (1999): pp. 125–133

87 Butler, Judith, *Gender Trouble*. New York: Routledge (1990), p. 139

88 Bial, Henry, 'Play', *The Performance Studies Reader*. Ed. Henry Bial. Routledge (2004; 2007), 135–136. p. 135.

89 Huzinga, Johan, *Homo Ludens: A Study of the Play Element in Culture*. Routledge (1949)

90 Aristotle, *Nicomachean Ethics*. Trans. WD Ross. Kitchener: Batoche, 1999. Book 2, Ch 1.